TENNIS :
A CUT ABOVE THE REST

TENNIS :
A CUT ABOVE THE REST
Chris Ronaldson

(IRONBARK)

RONALDSON PUBLICATIONS

First published in 1985 by Ronaldson Publications
www.ronaldsonpublications.co.uk
Second edition 1987
Third edition 1995
Fourth edition 1999
Fifth edition 2009

British Library Cataloguing in Publication Data
Ronaldson, Chris
    Tennis: A Cut Above The Rest
    1, Court tennis
    1. Title
    796.34 GV 1003

ISBN 978-0-9510251-1-6

Set in eleven on twelve point Baskerville
and printed on 115 g.s.m. Hello Silk by
Holywell Press Limited, 15-17 Kings Meadow,
Ferry Hinksey Road, Oxford OX2 0DP.

To Lesley

The author is indebted to Cliff Chetwood for his sponsorship of this book and for his encouragement

Photographs at Hampton Court Palace by Gracious Permission of Her Majesty The Queen

The great majority of other photographs by Noel Edwards

Diagrams by Lesley Ronaldson

Dust jacket from a painting by Shelly Bancroft

CONTENTS

LIST OF ILLUSTRATIONS

Page

FOREWORD

Chris Ronaldson has written a fascinating book. It falls into three sections. The first and second sections comprise a teaching manual, the former for beginners and the latter for established players. Both are full of wise advice, given from a long study of the game. The third section is an account of the author's tennis-playing career. All parts are enlivened by a sense of humour and many amusing anecdotes.

Chris is one of those players who not only have a natural talent but who devote long hours to studying the techniques of the game and to trying them out in practice. He has served tennis very well as a player, coach and administrator. He has now added another service in recording in writing his advice on playing methods distilled from his many years of experience.

We have all listened with interest and amusement to our professional friends telling tales of their past and wished that they could have been set down in writing. Chris has done just that and future players will read his stories with fascination. I only hope he does not lose too many friends in the process!

In the last paragraph he writes one sentence with which I profoundly agree. "A club can barely exist without a professional and I believe that the quality of professional drawn to tennis has a great deal to do with the health of the game." The health of tennis has been greatly enhanced by his own contribution to the game.

The Rt. Hon. The Lord Aberdare K.B.E.

INTRODUCTION

There are plenty of folk about who have difficulty avoiding boredom at the weekends. They wash their cars, potter about in their gardens, take their kids for walks, read their Sunday papers from cover to cover and doze off in front of their televisions after their Sunday lunches.

To me it is another world - and one which I crave. It seems that there are always half-a-dozen rackets to be repaired, a new set of balls to be covered, at least a score of names on my urgent correspondence list and countless other sundry items besides. I have never washed my car, nor done any gardening and my sons certainly do not receive enough paternal attention. Just when there appears to be a light at the end of the tunnel, a 'project' turns up. This could be a feasibility study for the construction of a new tennis court somewhere, a survey of local educational establishments that might be prepared to accept an unruly Ronaldson child or, most recently and most preposterously, the writing of a coaching book on tennis. It is at such times that one realises that the light at the end of the tunnel was not, in fact, the end of the tunnel, but a train approaching.

The pages that follow started as a pricking of my conscience, because there is no comprehensive coaching manual of tennis. My first idle doodlings were quite amusing, but that stage passed very quickly and soon the exercise became a fully-fledged obsession. Failed scientists (not to mention tennis professionals) are not normally noted for their literary talents and I have no illusions about the shortcomings of this book. Nevertheless, it is done; and I trust that it will serve its purpose.

The volume is divided into three parts. The first is an introduction to the game for those who know nothing, or next to nothing, about it. The second is a serious examination of the strokes and strategies of tennis for players wishing to improve their techniques. The final part was designed as a coaching section for advanced students. It does contain ideas and tips, but I have diluted the section with an account of my experiences within tennis, travelling the world and meeting some intriguing characters.

It should be noted that the advice contained herein is no substitute for personal tuition from a competent, experienced professional. The strokes and faults of different players are as diverse as their finger-prints and each deserves individual attention. In addition, no two professionals teach in precisely the same way, and I acknowledge that there is not universal acceptance of my methods.

My apologies to any who may be offended by my continuous use of the masculine gender when referring to an unspecified player or pupil. My sympathies also lie with left-handers, who have been discriminated against whenever a phrase such as 'the forehand corner' has been used because, for the sake of fluency, it has been assumed that the reader is right-handed.

Cliff Chetwood has sponsored and supported this venture, just as he sponsors and supports everything that goes on in the world of tennis, and I am most grateful to him.

Thanks are offered warmly to 'Reg' Routledge for providing some impetus at the beginning; to my sister Kathy and her husband James McNicoll and to Ronald Swash for proof-reading and advice; to Noel Edwards, Murray Glover and Stuart Routledge for their help with the photography; to my cousin Shelly Bancroft for her artistic dust-jacket; to John Pickering-Cail and Ruth Roberts for their technical know-how of word-processors and the world of printing; to my wife Lesley for her diagrams, love and patience; to Lachlan Deuchar for his sense of humour and for sewing my share of the balls during the bad times; and to Carolyn Welch for continually reminding me that I am a lousy writer.

Lord Aberdare is the leading authority and historian of the game of tennis and, such are his literary powers, he has managed to say a few kind words about this book in the preface. It adds a welcome touch of class and I am indebted to him for that.

Finally I must thank my father, Bruce Ronaldson, who has devoted more time to this undertaking than anybody. Without his unflagging support, typing, endless proof-reading and ability to tie up all the loose ends, the composition would surely have wound up as a hand-written bundle of papers at the bottom of my cupboard. For the prodigious efforts he has put in on my behalf, I will forgive him for the accursed, old-fashioned punctuation upon which he insists.

Hampton Court Palace
January, 1985

PREFACE TO THE FIFTH EDITION

The first edition of this book went on sale almost a quarter of a century ago, on the day I began a defence of my World Championship title against Wayne Davies, in March 1985.

As publishers, my father and I were delighted by the demand. We had plunged headlong into the venture without any real business plan – hoping for a profit but prepared to write off a loss for a time-consuming and absorbing new hobby. Production of the original manuscript had been reasonably hard work, proof-reading had been one long nightmare, but the publishing side had been interesting. Most of the latter proved to be fairly straightforward: discovering the ins and -outs of paper quality, point sizes, cover selection, British Library cataloguing, ISBN (numbering) and the laws of copyright. We were aiming for a product in which we could take some pride and, unconstrained by budgetary requirements, we managed to achieve our goal. We discovered that the real advantage held by large publishers lies not so much in their production expertise, as in their distribution and marketing network. They can't necessarily produce better volumes than their smaller competitors, but they can ship them out a lot faster.

In the absence of alternative coaching books we have come under pressure, on a number of occasions, to reprint even though, like its author, the work has aged somewhat. Most of the instructional sections are timeless and I have faith in their continuing value to students of the game, but the rambling reminiscences of Part Three come to a juddering halt in the mid-eighties. However, further reflections may be found in a short epilogue at the back of this fifth edition, the first to be produced in soft-back.

Tennis is played in a different way at the top level compared with twenty-five years ago, partly because of improvements in racket technology and partly because of the influence of an extraordinary world champion, Rob Fahey. Much of the current thinking about the game has changed. It is now many years since I have competed and, although some leading players continue to seek my advice, others would consider me passé. I'm sure you will benefit from reading these pages, but keep listening to your own coach as well.

Radley College
May 2009

PART ONE

CHAPTER 1

THE COURT AND EQUIPMENT

Tennis has an impressive pedigree - there are many fine books on that subject alone; and to my mind it provides a good example of evolution.

The general configuration of the court is reputed to have come from the cloisters of French monasteries, where the game is said to have originated. The popularity of the game reached a peak between 1550 and 1700 when there were many hundreds of courts in Paris alone. By and large, it seems that these courts were each owned by a 'maître paumier' and there were considerable variations in the dimensions and features to be found. Those were the days of genuine free enterprise and, if your court and balls were better than those of the next maître paumier's, then you got fat and he went broke. Thus it rapidly became established that the courts which provided the most pleasure, and the finest tests of skill, were large and equipped with penthouses, tambours, grilles and galleries, just as they are to be found today. No doubt the quality of the refreshment served 'après-jeu' by the good maître had something to do with it, and maybe even the shapeliness of his teenage daughter; but gradually a degree of standardisation evolved. Many novices today are amused by what they regard as the gimmicky aspects of the court, but they are all positive ingredients of a game which has lasted for many centuries.

Sadly, one observes that the evolution analogy continues and that now the tennis court bears a strong resemblance to the dinosaur: too large and inflexible to thrive in today's climate of cheaper and simpler alternatives, such as lawn tennis - its own descendant - the demand for quick returns in sport participation, huge and luxurious spectator facilities, television and big money sponsorship.

None of this detracts from its magnificence! To this day tennis remains unique among active sports, as a game which presents a great physical challenge to the young, a demanding test of skill for the connoisseurs (it has been referred to as chess on a court) and yet which encourages older players to continue working at the game, because the development of court-craft can compensate, at least to some extent, for the athletic decline.

What do we have? Well, the net divides the court, service end from hazard end. It also penalises the shot that goes too low and encourages players to aim cross-court, since it is two feet lower in the middle than at the sides. The penthouses at the back of each end of the court penalise

1

the shot that goes too high, for the ball usually rebounds from them slowly and innocuously, and the opponent assumes command of the rest. Correct elevation of shot is therefore vital.

The basic and sound tactic of most players is to try to gain, and then to retain, the service end as much as possible and to plug away at the grille and tambour. Beginners are well advised to adopt this policy at first - at least until their own strengths and weaknesses have become apparent. The low shot from the service end into the grille corner will yield a high percentage of winners.

At the back of the service end yawns the dedans, inviting you to try for an outright winner; but beware - until you are experienced, the dedans can be a trap. Should you be successful in your attempt to force for the dedans, then you have won the point, to be sure, but you are still stuck down at the hazard (and probably losing) end. Too often you will find that you are not successful - many forces travel too high and are dispatched by your opponent; many accurate forces can be safely volleyed back and, at this early stage in your career, you are not developing the right swing by excessive forcing.

Before leaving the court, note the multitude of angles and possibilities and try to accept that, no matter how rich your talents are and how flawless you intend your technique to be, your knowledge of all the combinations of these angles and possibilities will take no little time to accumulate, for no one masters tennis without massive experience.

A tennis ball is solid and is made by hand today in much the same way as it has been made for the last few centuries - only the materials have changed a little. New balls, in Britain in 1985, are made by winding thirteen yards of cotton webbing round and round an old wine cork that has been cut up and reshaped.

This core is then bound tightly in an exact pattern with a linen thread; and covered with a woollen felt, which is sewn up with a finer linen thread.

A set of seventy-two such balls will last for about one hundred and sixty hours of play, after which the balls will be stripped of their old covers, re-bound and re-covered.

The finished ball is about two and a half inches in diameter, a little over two and a half ounces in weight and should have a bounce of around twenty-three per cent (cf. a lawn tennis ball which should rebound

The Equipment for Making Balls

about fifty-five per cent). Statistics apart, this is a very heavy ball for a racket sport. Its bounce is low and comparatively fast and it demands careful stroking. Its most distinctive characteristic, however, is its susceptibility to spin. You can adjust to the low bounce and the weight of the ball fairly readily, but learning how to apply spin properly, and how to read your opponent's little chops and slices, will take a good number of court hours. It is not enough to know how the ball will react off the different surfaces: it has to be so well known that it is instinctive, so that your positioning may be rapid, efficient and natural.

At first grasp, the racket feels rather clumsy and it certainly takes some getting used to. It is twenty-six inches long and weighs some fifteen ounces. It is a solid piece of equipment, but then it needs to be, in order to deal with heavy balls moving at high speeds. The sturdiness is also a safeguard against breakage, particularly when mis-hitting volleys and thwacking the racket against the walls.

Over the years there has been considerable development of the racket; but that is a subject all by itself and will not receive proper treatment here. One aspect that has not changed however, is the asymmetric face

3

of the racket. The game in France is still known as Jeu de Paume - game of the palm - and today the racket is still shaped like an opened hand with the fingers spread. It has a small face and the asymmetry has two advantages: it allows the player to get the centre of the face (as defined by the extension of the handle) closer to the floor; and it facilitates the action of cutting (i.e. imparting backspin to) the ball because, after striking this 'centre', there is more space for the ball to slide across the strings above this point.

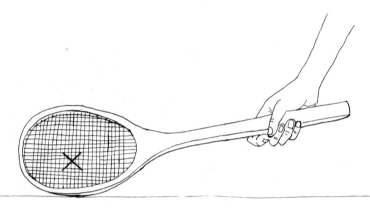

CHAPTER 2

THE GRIP

For the standard grip, the racket should be taken by the throat with the left hand, as shown below. Three fingers of the right hand should be placed under the handle, leaving the heel of the hand about three inches from the butt. The thumb and forefinger are then placed either side of the handle, and minor adjustments are made for comfort, keeping the fingers fairly well spread.

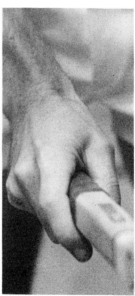

In this position the racket is a natural extension of the hand, and it may be used for both forehand and backhand strokes by rotating the wrist.

The size of the handle and the covering material thereon is a matter of personal preference. To a large extent, you get used to what you have. Many players have used different grips with great success, and there is much scope for individual variations. It is more important for you to have a comfortable grip than a correct one. Your choice of grip, the handle shape and size, and its covering can depend on your physique, temperament, susceptibility to tennis elbow, sweatiness of palm or anything else. I use a handle four and a half inches in circumference and bound in leather, and I lengthen my grip for backhands, while shortening it considerably for most services.

CHAPTER 3

THE READY POSITION

When playing a rest you should, whenever possible, take up a central position about six feet from the back of the court, slightly crouched forward, and with your racket hand in front of you at about waist height.

If you are receiving service, then you should be even closer to the back wall, standing at about the centre line and facing the winning gallery, for you know that the service will come from that general direction. Classically, you should also be 'stooped' - bent forward from the waist as you await the service, and your left foot should be slightly advanced.

CHAPTER 4

ELEMENTARY COACHING

When giving a novice his first lesson, I invariably start by hitting a basket of balls to him. This allows him time to get acquainted with the racket and the way the ball bounces, and gives me a chance to assess his natural ability, footwork and stroking tendencies.

The next basket of balls is almost always taken down to the hazard end where I roll the balls off the service penthouse so that they drop on to the forehand (of a right-hander) as a simulated slow and easy service. Thus the first stroke learned by the pupil is the forehand return of serve (or backhand if he is a left-hander). The importance of this stroke can scarcely be overstated. In general, the configuration of the court aids the server and once a rest gets going, he is the favourite to win it. The one major asset the receiver has is that he usually gets first crack at an easy ball, as most services can be attacked. Therefore it is essential that he takes full advantage of this, by learning a sound stroke that will keep the server under pressure and yield a high percentage of good chases.

To this end, the two corner-stones around which I build my instructions of this stroke are: firstly, that the pupil should position himself so that he has to reach towards the net in order to strike the ball and, secondly, that the path of the racket during the stroke should be in a generally downward direction, as well as forward.

These points require amplification. At lawn tennis, the forehand ground stroke should be produced in such a way as to strike the ball when it is at a point in front of and between the feet, and at squash the

The Point of Contact for the Forehand

8

ball should be taken rather nearer the back foot; but at tennis the forehand ground stroke should be played opposite the leading foot, or slightly in front of it. For lawn tennis players this approximates to the low volley, and squash players can get the feel for it by imitating drop shots.

I will use the same comparisons to illustrate the path the racket takes during the stroke. At lawn tennis, one is coached to start the forward swing from a low position, in order to be able to hit up and over the ball with the racket finishing high. This will impart the desired topspin. At squash, the back-swing is high and the racket head then describes a rough circle, striking the ball at the low point and finishing at the top again. This gives power and at the same time minimises danger to the opponent because the whole stroke is compact. Well, at tennis the stroke should start high, follow a straight line to and through the ball, and then finish low. This stroke is the recommended one because of the safety inherent in hitting along the line of the ball, and because it tends to give backspin to the ball, which will cause it to keep low at the other end of the court.

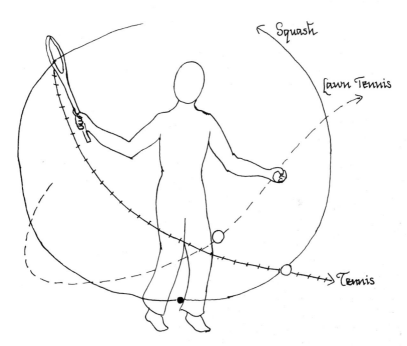

The Arcs of Various Swings

9

The average student finds this stroke rather foreign; but after a few minutes he should have a mental picture of what he is trying to do, and the semblance of a return of serve becomes apparent.

The next quarter of an hour or so is usually devoted to the rudiments of serving, for once the student has both a service and a return of serve, then he is in a position to play a game, no matter how badly.

The first lesson in serving is a defensive one - how to produce deliveries that do not give your opponent an easy line of attack - and the best way to achieve this objective is to make sure that your length of service is good. All the fancy spins and subtleties can come later.

For a beginner, service variations fall into two categories: those which strike the service wall above the penthouse and those which do not.

Taking the latter case first, the pupil is asked to stand half-way between the side penthouse and centre line at around chase three, and then strike the ball so that it rolls or bobbles along the side penthouse, before falling off as near to the nick on the grille wall as possible. (The nick is the junction between the wall and the floor.) The trick is to balance the strength of your service against the angle of the penthouse in order to produce the correct length. After a score or so of practice balls, it is usually possible to get a 'feel' for this.

The other service is given from much the same place and involves hitting the ball with a little backspin directly up to the service wall, about three feet above the penthouse and a little more than half-way along it. From there, the ball should bounce on the penthouse before dropping down towards the nick on the grille wall.

It is worth stressing at this point that the service to be avoided, at all costs, is the one that runs right along the side penthouse and then onto the grille penthouse. This happens mostly when the service is over-hit and the result is a very easy ball, which your opponent can dispose of at his will.

The first lesson concludes with a quick examination of the rules (a précis of which appears below) followed by a short game, in which the novice tries desperately to put together the pieces of advice he has received about how to score, how to play the strokes, and what tactics to employ. It is a fairly daunting task and few accomplish it without embarrassment, but I find that it usually accentuates the challenge that the newcomer feels from this demanding game.

Subsequent lessons, like subsequent chapters of this book, are much more specific about coaching techniques.

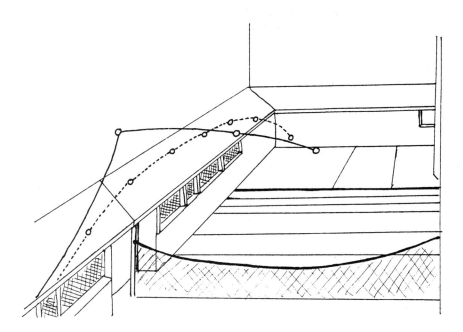

Paths of Elementary Services

CHAPTER 5

THE RULES

This section is not designed to be a complete exposition of the laws of tennis, but rather a set of guidelines on how the game is played.

As you enter the *court* the *service end* is on the right hand side of the *net* and the *hazard end* is to the left. *Service* is always delivered from the service end - in fact from behind the third line from the net (known as the *second gallery line*).

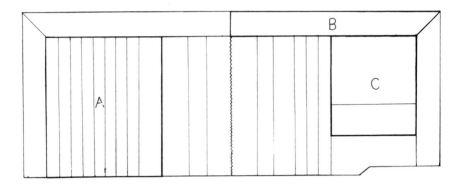

So you may serve from anywhere within area A. After leaving the server's racket, the ball must touch the *penthouse* on the hazard side (area B) although it is allowed to hit the penthouse on the service side and/or the wall above the side penthouse as well. Finally the ball must land in area C on the hazard side, unless the receiver chooses to volley it. The server is allowed a second service if the first service is a fault.

The ball is then in play and a *rest* (which is a rally) ensues. Strokes may be played directly over the net, or along the penthouses, or off any wall below the out-of-court lines, providing the ball crosses the net. You may volley or you may hit the ball after it has bounced once on the floor (regardless of how many other surfaces the ball hits before or after the bounce).

Many points are scored from your opponent's errors: when, through pressure applied by you, or inaccuracy on his part, he hits the ball into the net or out of play. However there are three *winning openings* where outright aces can be scored.

The first is the *dedans*, which is the large net at the back of the service end.

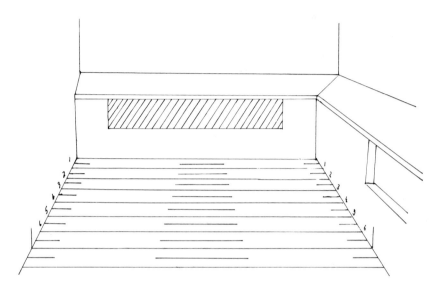

The Service End

The second is the *grille* and the third is the *winning gallery* and both of these are located at the hazard end. In front of the grille stands the *tambour*, which is a buttress that generally aids the cause of the server.

A ball entering one of these winning openings, either directly or by bouncing off a wall, a penthouse or the floor, will score a point for the striker.

The scoring system is basically the same as for lawn tennis. To win a game a player must win a minimum of four points (15,30,40, game) and be two or more points ahead of his adversary. If the score reaches 40-all, deuce is called and that game continues until one player is two points ahead. The first player to win six games wins the set and, to do so, it is not necessary to be two games ahead (i.e. if the score reaches five games all, the eleventh game is decisive). All of the above is fairly straightforward, but the following rules require more concentration:

1. It is the score of the player who won the last point (not necessarily the server) that is called first. Thus whoever wins the first point of the game, the score must be 15-love and this can be 15-love to the server or

13

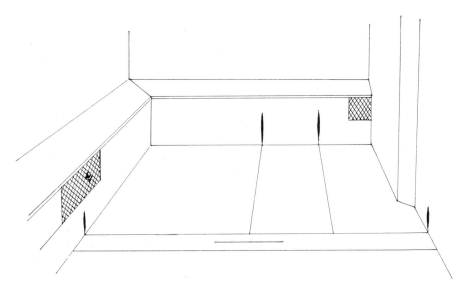

The Hazard End

to the receiver. If the score is called '30-40' this means that the player who was 15-40 behind (at whichever end he is) has just won the point to reach 30-40.

2. If either player hits the ball but fails to keep it in play, or if one of the winning openings is struck, a point is *always* scored. This is also true if the player at the hazard end allows the ball to take a second bounce, and that bounce is within the area between the service line and the back wall at the hazard end.

3. If the ball bounces a second time on the floor anywhere else on the court (irrespective of any walls it may strike before that bounce) or enters one of the *side galleries* other than the winning gallery, a *chase* is scored. If the second bounce is, for instance, on the line marked 5, then it is called 'Chase five'; if the ball enters the last gallery it is called 'Chase the last gallery.'

4. Consider a chase at the service end - say, chase four on the floor. This means that the player at the hazard end (let's call him Bill) has struck the ball so that its second bounce has landed on the chase 4 line. The server (whom we shall call Ben) has been unable to reach the ball, or has missed it completely, or has deliberately left it. When this happens no

14

point is scored, but a *chase is set* and this chase is significant on two counts.

First of all, it means that Bill has won the right to change to the service end - not necessarily immediately, but at least within the next few points. This is important because, in this asymmetric court, most points are won by the server.

Secondly Ben, having conceded a chase of four, will be required, on changing ends, to play the next rest in such a way that all his shots would, if allowed to do so, take their second bounces nearer the back wall than the 4 line. In effect, by setting a chase, Bill has set a 'standard' of four and Ben, having conceded the chase, is required to change ends and to attempt to beat that standard.

5. How does all this affect the conventional score? It is important to remember that when a chase is set, the score does not change. A chase is a point half played: it is held in abeyance until the players change ends and only then is 'played off' to completion. If the new receiver, Ben, beats the chase by forcing an error, or by striking the ball into the dedans, or by hitting a shot that takes a second bounce on the floor between the back wall and (in this example) the 4 line, then he wins the point that was held in abeyance.

If, however, Ben plays a shot which is going to bounce for a second time on the floor between the net and the 4 line, the new server, Bill, should allow it to do so and would win the point because Ben has failed to *beat the chase*. For his part Bill may also win the point by forcing an error, or by striking the ball into the grille or into the winning gallery, or by hitting any shot over the net that Ben does not reach, including hitting the ball into any of the galleries at the hazard end. In these cases Ben is deemed to have failed to beat the chase (of four). Thus the point which was held in abeyance is determined.

Should the second bounce fall exactly on the same mark as previously recorded (chase four) then 'Chase off' is called and neither player scores a point. The score remains unchanged and the chase is discarded.

6. When do the players change ends? The answer is never, unless there is a chase; and then only when one of the two following circumstances obtain:

(a) The score is game point (40-love, 40-15, 40-30 or advantage) and there is a chase outstanding, set at that or any previous stage during the game.

(b) There are two chases.

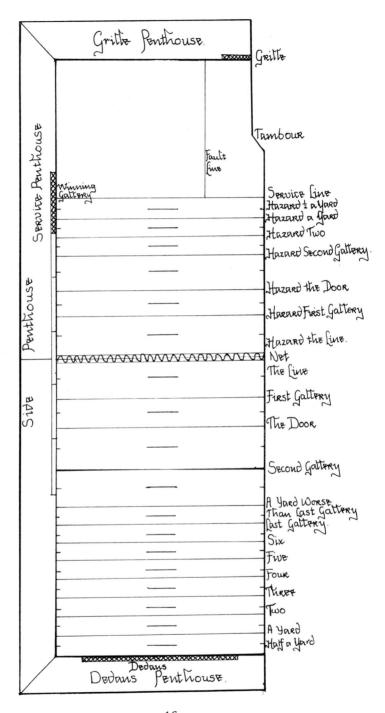

Grille Penthouse.

Grille

Tambour

Service Penthouse

Fault line

Winning Gallery

Service Line
Hazard ½ a Yard
Hazard a Yard
Hazard Two
Hazard Second Gallery.

Penthouse

Hazard the Door

Hazard First Gallery

Side

Hazard the Line.
Net
The Line

First Gallery

The Door

Second Gallery

A Yard Worse
Than Last Gallery
Last Gallery.
Six
Five
Four
Three
Two
A Yard
Half a Yard

Dedans
Dedans Penthouse.

If the score is, for instance, 40-15 (to either player) when a chase is set, then immediately the conditions for (a) apply and the players change ends; but if the score is only 15-all when the chase is set then the players continue at their respective ends (mentally storing the chase) until one player reaches 40, whereupon they change ends - for reason (a) - or until, when the score is say, 30-all, a second chase is set whereupon the players change ends immediately - for reason (b).

NOTES

(A) When the players change ends at game point and a chase, the chase has to be played off immediately and, even if the server delivers a double fault, that is the end of that chase. If there are two chases at the change, then they are played off in chronological order on the first two points after the change.

(B) Whether or not a chase is beaten affects only the outcome of the point held in abeyance. Beating a chase does not entitle that player to return to the service end. To do this he must, at a later stage, set a chase of his own.

(C) If a ball enters a side gallery other than the winning gallery, it sets a chase by the name of that gallery and equivalent to the line on the floor underneath that gallery.

(D) If a ball were to fall (second bounce) just nearer the back wall than, for instance, the 4 line, it is called 'Chase better than four'. If it falls just nearer the net than that 4 line, it is called 'Chase worse than four'.

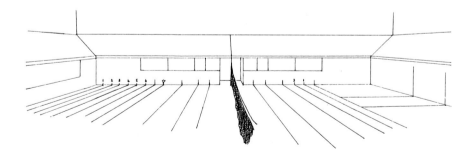

The Court from the Main Wall

(E) Hazard chases are chases set on the hazard side of the net by the server. These occur only occasionally, when the server strikes the ball into one of the side galleries at the hazard end (other than the winning gallery); or when the server hits such a poor shot that its second bounce is between the net and the service line. This is normally bad tactics on the part of the server because it means that, by setting a chase, albeit on the hazard side, he will lose the service end during that game.

Hazard chases count just as ordinary chases in terms of when ends are changed, and they are played off in the same way, except that it is the (new) server who has to beat the hazard chase after changing ends.

PART TWO

CHAPTER 6

THE FOREHAND FLOOR SHOT

Strokes in this sport are divided primarily into two categories: those which are taken before the back wall, and those where the ball is allowed to strike the back wall before being played.

The former are called floor shots and the technique for playing the forehand floor shot is what follows. (It is assumed that you have been playing for a while and that you have decided it is time to get down to it properly.)

Take a basket of balls to the hazard end and throw one of them on to the side penthouse. When it rolls off, allow it to bounce once and then strike it over the net. Very well, what we want to know is what happened to your feet, left knee, waist, shoulders, right elbow, right wrist, racket head and racket face while that instinctive swing took place. Now let's make a comparison with what should have happened, starting with the *feet*. They should begin by positioning you accurately with several small bouncing steps. Then, just before impact, your left foot should move away from the right foot, along the line that you intend to hit the ball, with the toes pointing towards the winning gallery (and, incidentally, the ball should be on a line between the left foot and that gallery when you strike it). This means that the left foot should finish in a position such that, should you play your stroke and miss, the ball would travel just past the outside of your left foot - i.e. you were well behind the ball.

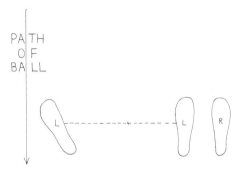

Forehand Footwork

This is the footwork that batsmen adopt when playing off the front foot at cricket, and this is because tennis and cricket have in common a heavy ball. In these cases, it is important to have one's weight moving into the stroke - unlike squash, for example, where the most serious consideration is racket head speed and control, and one is encouraged

21

to strike the light squash ball with the racket moving across the line of the feet.

In the act of taking your final stride your left leg should be bending so that, by the end of the swing, your *left knee* is almost forming a right-angle. This means that you have your weight moving down as well as forward, and the cut shot you are playing will have more bite. Make sure that you finish on balance, that you do not fall out of the shot and that you stay low for a fraction of a second after completing the follow-through.

Stooping is an old-fashioned idea in tennis and is a good one. Try to develop the habit of bending slightly forward from the *waist* in between strokes and when moving to the ball. This will increase the likelihood of your being on your toes and be of value should sudden movement be necessary.

There are two common faults relating to the *shoulders* while playing forehand strokes. The first is the tendency of the right shoulder to drop below the left during the stroke; the second is for the left shoulder to open out before contact is made. The first is wrong because it means you are hitting *against* the left side instead of *with* it; and in both cases

Incorrect Technique for Shoulders

22

you are losing power and control because the bulk of your weight is moving in the wrong direction.

The shoulders should remain level with each other and rotate together through about ninety degrees.

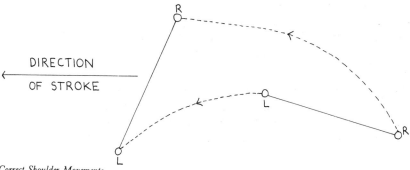

Correct Shoulder Movements

At the start of the swing, the arm should be well bent at the *elbow* and relaxed. At the finish the arm should be almost straight, the straightening process having been delayed as long as possible. A tennis stroke is much more akin to a chopping action than to a slinging one.

Hold your racket out in front of you, its face parallel with the net. There are three things you can do with it simply by moving your *wrist:*
a)   you can raise and lower the head in a vertical plane;
b)   you can move the head to left and right in a slapping action;
c)   you can rotate the head through about one hundred and eighty degrees (this is actually a pronation of the forearm, but it is more logical here to include it under the concept of wrist movements).

In lawn tennis action (c) is the one used most, and in squash it is action (b); but at this game you should try to minimise both of these. The only one which is encouraged is the one described in (a) and even that has to be strictly controlled. At the top of the stroke (for with bent elbow that is where you start) the wrist should be partially cocked - i.e. the hand should be making an angle of about thirty degrees with the forearm. The wrist should remain locked in this position until just before you strike the ball, whereupon the hand drops in a disciplined fashion until it is in line with the forearm.

Let us now concern ourselves with the *racket head.* This should commence at a position about a foot above and a foot away from your right shoulder, and descend diagonally forwards as you step into the ball, with your arm gradually straightening. After contact, this direction of the racket head is continued until it is only a few inches

The Forehand from the Side Penthouse

Preparation

Contact

Follow-through

25

from the floor, whereupon it should sweep round in front of you, pointing towards the net. A most important part of this stroke is the beginning. If your racket is not up there early enough, it is very difficult to control your wrist movements and all sorts of errors creep in. The stroke should then be played at a steady pace with a smooth follow-through. Many players have trouble keeping their rackets low at the end of the stroke, but forming this habit is important, or you will find yourself 'lifting' the ball over the net with the wrong trajectory and little effectiveness.

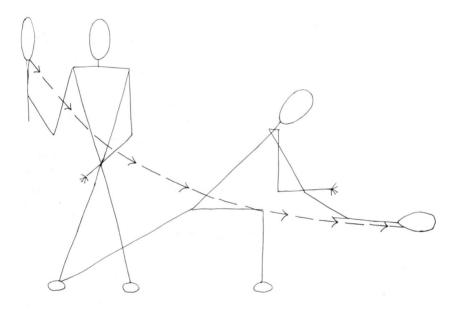

Racket Head Path

As you hit the ball, the lower edge of the *racket face* should be very slightly nearer the net than the upper edge - i.e. the racket face should be slightly 'open'. Therefore, at both ends of the stroke, the face should be in positions that will result in this correct angle being produced at impact with minimal wrist movement. Normally the lower edge of the racket will lead into the shot from start to finish.

So - now you know what to do and you have about two seconds to get it all right as the next ball rolls off that side penthouse. How do you fit those eight separate items of technique together?

While the ball is still up there you should be moving into position - bobbing about on your toes, slightly stooped, with your racket already up, elbow bent and wrist cocked. Should you be turned to stone at this point in time, the ball would roll past you, about three feet to your left as you face the side wall.

Let us assume that you are not turned to stone but remain in dynamic athletic form. As the ball is dropping to the floor you are making your final preparations. You take your last pace down the court with the left foot, toe pointing towards the winning gallery. Your shoulders rotate slightly clockwise (looking from above), and your right arm remains disciplined, but relaxed and bent.

The ball rises to the top of its bounce and you strike. Your weight shifts forward on to the left leg and down as you bend the left knee. Your racket is also moving forwards and down, not too fast and with the lower edge of the frame just leading. You are still facing the side wall and your arm is gradually unbending as it crosses your body. Your wrist allows the racket face to move down the back of the ball.

Now the ball is well on its way to chase better than a yard, your opponent is floundering and the packed gallery is roaring its approval. You, on the other hand, are concentrating on your follow-through. Still bent low, you allow your shoulders to swing through at last, wrist under control, racket head sweeping past close to the ground. Almost all your weight is on your left foot and the right foot has risen so that only the big toe is touching the ground. You are perfectly balanced because you have not attempted to hit the ball too hard.

The forehand floor shot and, in particular, the return of serve are of paramount importance at tennis, and I suggest that a few minutes in the living room with an imaginary racket would be of benefit. A century ago an aspiring beginner would be required to practise this stroke for months on end before ever he faced an adversary, so that under pressure the instinctive swing would be the correct one.

It may well be that your aspirations are not that high, you do not have that much available time, or you are numbed by the complexity of this seemingly unnatural stroke. Do not despair, the vast majority are with you. Some players have coped very well with improvised and incorrect strokes; others have learned the classic stroke gradually. Do, however, start with the following maxims:

1. Your racket must be up early, with your wrist firm.
2. You should attempt to hit the ball when it is slightly nearer the net than your leading foot.

The Forehand Floor Shot

I must emphasise here that the perfect stroke we have just been through in detail is the one that should be used to play a ball rolling or bouncing innocuously from the penthouse. There are slight modifications to be made if the ball is coming towards you over the net.

You will normally be facing your opponent as he strikes the ball. As soon as you realise that your next stroke will be a forehand floor shot, you should prepare for it by moving nimbly into position and by turning your left shoulder so that you are facing the side wall. Your final step, on to your left foot and towards the net, should be a large one. As you play your stroke you should push your wrist forwards, so that the racket head tends to follow the ball rather than circling round in front of your legs. When practising this stroke myself, I improve my timing by telling myself to adopt a three-stage sequence: forwards, pause, punch. I try to reach forwards to meet the ball, then delay for a fraction of a second and, finally, play a sharp, punching stroke at it. You should aim straight for one of the two corners at the opposite end of the court and strike the ball firmly, so that it pitches just short of the back wall nick and cuts down quickly off that wall. This is not a classic length of shot, but it is the most effective one for this type of stroke, which is difficult to control in terms of length and which carries backspin.

The easier and slower the ball, the more inclined you should be to play it as a ball from the side penthouse. However, if it is faster and/or lower, you should reduce your back-swing and curtail your follow-through accordingly. For the very fast, low ball the racket should start at only waist height and the ball should be punched, so that the racket stops only a few inches after impact. For these difficult balls, you should also be aware of trying to keep the swing as nearly as possible in a straight line through the path of the ball, as this will help to reduce errors.

Frequently, you will be required to play forehand floor shots when the ball is well wide of you. In these cases, when you are doing well to reach

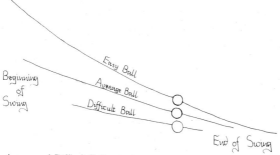

Strokes for Easy, Average and Difficult Balls

29

the ball at all, and it is impossible to get your feet in a line parallel to the intended direction of the stroke, you should strike the ball with your left foot forward.

CHAPTER 7

THE BACKHAND FLOOR SHOT

If you are seriously interested in learning to play a correct backhand I
shall make two assumptions. The first is that you have read the section
on the forehand floor shot and the second is that you are not just a
pretty face - you can remember the principles expounded about the
forehand and apply them in reverse on this other wing. What I shall
deal with here are the differences between the two strokes, thereby
avoiding a fair measure of repetition. If you are indeed just a pretty face
then don't worry, because no-one will be looking at your backhand
anyway.

Throw a few balls on to the side penthouse at the service end, so that
they drop from there to the floor on your backhand. The first major
adjustment that you have to make is in your positioning relative to the
ball. Your racket should be regarded as an extended hand and it swings
from your right shoulder. When playing a forehand, this right shoulder
is behind the body, whereas on the backhand it leads the body. Thus, in
order to get the same movement into the ball and the same angle on

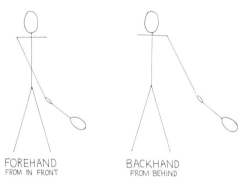

FOREHAND
FROM IN FRONT

BACKHAND
FROM BEHIND

Relative Position of Racket Head to Feet

Backhand Footwork

31

The Backhand from the Side Penthouse

Preparation

Contact

Follow-through

your arm at impact, you need to start a foot or so further behind the ball (i.e. nearer the back wall) than you would have done for the forehand.

In addition, for reasons described later, you should be hitting most of your backhands cross-court and this angling is assisted by having to stretch forwards for the ball.

There are a couple of consequences to bear in mind. Stretching forward for the ball, as you are now doing, tends to make some players become too square on to the net, so that they end up pushing at the ball instead of stroking it. In order to prevent this, try to ensure that your torso still faces the side wall during your final preparations and that your shoulders are turned away from the ball. The toes of your leading (right) foot should still point toward the place where your racket and the ball will meet but, because the ball is further forward, this means that your toes will point more to the first gallery than the last gallery (assuming that you are at the service end).

The other difference in technique concerns weight of shot. There are three ways in which you should be bringing your body weight into effect: by stepping into the ball; by bending with the stroke; and by rotating the upper body on impact. These three actions are consecutive in that order and we have already dealt with the first two of them. The third, the rotation from the hips, occurs naturally in the forehand provided that you are correctly positioned and relaxed. As you swing your arm you are obliged to turn with the shot so as to remain comfortable. Not so with the backhand - it is perfectly natural for the right arm to move away from the body and follow through by itself. Provided that you are getting the basics right you can play excellent shots like this, but you will get an extra bit of bite if you can add a little rotational momentum as well.

At the top of your back-swing, you will notice that your shoulders are hunched together. Well, try to keep the shoulders hunched for the duration of the swing. The easy way to get it right is to adopt the habit of starting the stroke with your hands together, and ensuring that the left hand stays close to the right (without touching it or the racket) until the end of the follow-through. If you do this, you will find that the left side of your body has been dragged round and is adding its weight to the shot.

Not Recommended:
No Upper Body Rotation

For the easy backhand floor shot, the racket head should commence behind the left ear and swing down and round to a position where the racket points towards the tambour (for a stroke played at the service end). The more difficult the shot is, the lower the starting point should be, the shorter the follow-through and the straighter the line of the stroke, just the same as for the forehand.

Once again, if you feel that all this is too much to swallow at one go, then the essentials to concentrate on are your position relative to the ball and the raising of your racket into place well before the start of the stroke.

The Backhand Floor Shot

CHAPTER 8

STROKES OFF THE SIDE WALL

If the ball strikes the back wall before the side wall you should play it as a back wall shot, a description of which follows shortly.

If the ball strikes the side wall before the floor, then you should play it as an ordinary floor shot, but paying particular attention to your footwork and ensuring that you turn your leading shoulder towards the ball as it approaches.

The difficult ball to play is the one that hits the floor before the side wall and which would die short of the back wall. When dealing with this stroke you should keep your head down and concentrate on hitting a slow, flat shot parallel to the side wall. Stay low at the end of the stroke and make your follow-through even more abbreviated than with a normal floor shot. Where possible, your feet should be equidistant from the side wall.

Backhand off Side Wall

CHAPTER 9

THE FOREHAND STROKE OFF THE BACK WALL

In dealing with this shot I will assume that the stroke you are intending to play off the back wall is a floor shot - in other words, a ball of good length and with some backspin that strikes the floor before the back wall. Forcing for the openings will be covered later.

Balls rebound from the back wall in an infinite variety of ways, depending on pace, trajectory, length, spin, angle and the order in which they strike the different surfaces. What follows is therefore necessarily a series of generalisations on how to play these balls.

The first essential is to learn to raise your racket into position well in advance. The position I recommend is the one shown below. Note that the racket head is between elbow and shoulder height, and that the head of the racket is laid back.

There are many advantages in learning this discipline. It usually eliminates the wristy flick at the back of the swing that afflicts the strokes of those who do not prepare early. It is also a natural starting-place for a stroke that is intended to impart backspin; whereas, if the racket

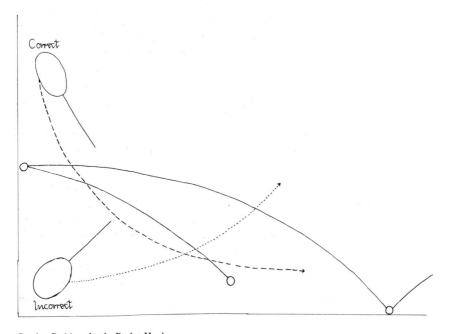

Starting Positions for the Racket Head

approaches the ball from underneath, it is obliged either to lift the ball over the net with no spin, or else to give it overspin in order to keep it low. Most importantly, this is the best racket position from which to begin the stroke if the ball proves to be difficult. The reaction of most players, when required to take an awkward ball off the back wall, is to drop the racket underneath it and to attempt to scoop it out. This not only produces a defensive return, if successful, but is actually less safe anyway.

As you can see from the diagram above, if the racket starts above the ball, it follows the path of the ball quite closely for a while and the striker has an extended period of time in which to make contact. By contrast, if the racket starts below the ball, then the racket and ball are moving along lines which cross and timing would have to be perfect. The latter is clearly more difficult and, as it is less effective anyway, there is little to be said for it.

The second point to concentrate on is footwork. This is a subject which needs sub-division and I start by stressing that you should take as many steps as you can fit in. If you feel you are in the right place already then jump up and down on the spot and, above all, do not take your final pace until the last possible moment. The reason is that no matter how correctly you think you have judged the ball, it can still deviate a few inches from the path you have mentally selected for it. If you are still moving then, instinctively, your last step will make at least part of the necessary adjustment; whereas if you have committed your leading foot to its final position and your weight is on that foot, then you are going to have to make that adjustment by lunging, or with a wristy flick, and the result will be unreliable, at best. You may glare at your opponent for the mis-hit he must have made, which caused you to mis-read the spin; or you may think foul thoughts about the professional who produced those balls, which must be square, but the real problem lies underneath your shoelaces.

In addition to this rather general piece of advice, there is a particular pattern of footwork which should be learned for back wall shots. The general rule is to move in the same direction as the ball, in as far as that is possible. Thus, when you elect to let your opponent's shot go to the back wall, you should then move across to the line of the ball in such a way that you finish closer to the back wall than usual and with your weight on your back foot. Depending on the rebound characteristics of the ball you should then take one, three or five steps towards the net, moving parallel to the line of the ball, two or three feet from it. You

The Forehand Stroke off the Back Wall

Preparation

40

Contact

Follow-through

41

should finish on balance, with your weight on your front (left) foot and with your back foot touching the ground at the toe.

Apart from the fine tuning that these steps make to your eventual position, they are important because they slow the ball down in relation to you yourself. This slower ball will be easier to stroke with the long, smooth swing that is required and which is described below.

This pattern of footwork is best developed by rolling balls off the back penthouse. When each is about to leave the penthouse, you should take one step back towards the back wall with your right foot and then, immediately, three paces forward, keeping the ball opposite you. This movement is a sideways one, made by opening, closing and re-opening your legs, and should end with you playing your shot just after you have taken the last of your steps, which is on to your left foot. With a little practice you can then use this footwork for balls coming off the back wall as well as off the back penthouse. Most beginners start by moving the wrong way, or the right way at the wrong time and it requires some perseverance.

The final directive to the feet is that they should normally point to where the ball is at any given time. As the ball passes you on its way to the back wall, in the course of your movements you should angle your feet (and your trunk) so that you turn, first towards the rear and then back more to the front again as the ball rebounds from the wall.

Far too many players have no conception that the stroke used to play balls off the back wall should be quite dissimilar to that used for floor shots. There are five major aspects of technique which are completely different for the two strokes:

1. Balls on the floor should be taken a few inches in front of your leading foot, if on the forehand side. Those off the back wall should be struck when the ball is between your two feet.

2. Floor shots should be struck with the racket face almost closed (vertical) whereas back wall strokes should be made with a more open face.

3. When the ball is to be played as it comes towards you from the net, you should bend your knees while in the act of playing the shot. By contrast, as soon as you decide to let a ball go to the back wall, you should bend immediately and conduct the rest of your preparations in the resultant crouched position, staying low as you play your stroke.

4. Given a choice, which doesn't happen very frequently, you should strike a floor shot as high off the ground as is possible and comfortable.

Conversely, off the back wall you should normally allow the ball to fall almost to the floor before contact. This appears hard to justify, at first, but allowing the ball to drop gives you precious fractions of a second in which to assess its difficulty, determine your strategy and maximise your control. This is one of the reasons why a novice seems to snatch at all his back wall strokes, whereas the master gives the impression that he has all the time in the world and can disguise his intentions.

5. The final characteristic where the two strokes are at variance is the length of the follow-through. Off the floor this should be short and crisp, while off the back wall it should be long, low and smooth.

When you get right down to the bones of it, the floor shot should be cut, whereas the back wall shot should be sliced.

A cut shot is produced by bringing the racket face down across the back of the ball, which should then fly low and fast with plenty of backspin. It will bounce relatively high off the floor and come down sharply off the back wall. By contrast, a sliced shot is played by moving the racket face almost horizontally along the underside of the ball. This also produces backspin but the ball will travel more slowly, appearing to float. Its bounce on the floor will be lower than that of the cut shot, and it will bite down less severely off the back wall.

Tennis is a difficult game: this must be recognised and techniques must be adopted which increase the chances of good contact between racket and ball. This is why we play strokes with a minimum of follow-through for balls taken off the floor, because the slow-moving racket head has more chance of being in the right place at the right time than a fast-moving one, which is there and gone in a flash. Off the back wall the best chance of controlled contact is for the racket and ball to be moving in the same direction for the maximum length of time. Hence the need for a long, smooth stroke that guides the ball to its destination.

With practice you will find that the back wall shot is much easier to control than the floor shot. This being so, you can aim for the 'classic' length and line, whereby the ball lands for the first time at chase six (or equivalent at the hazard end) then strikes the side wall between chase three and chase four, and dies as it hits the back wall.

CHAPTER 10

THE BACKHAND STROKE OFF THE BACK WALL

This stroke is essentially the same as the one for the forehand, just described, and my comments will relate only to those elements which are different. The correct position to take the ball, relative to yourself, is when it is opposite your right foot, or slightly in front if the intended direction of the shot is cross-court.

Some players have difficulty ascertaining the degree to which they should open the face of the racket. As a rough guide you should feel that, with a normal grip, the back of your hand is facing the ceiling.

Finally, when turning to play the stroke off the back wall you should pay attention to the movements of your shoulders. Before you make contact you should be showing your right shoulder blade to your opponent. By the end of the swing your trunk should have rotated through some ninety degrees and, although it is not vital, I recommend that you attempt to finish with both arms relaxed and extended towards your foe.

The Backhand Stroke off the Back Wall

Preparation

Contact

Follow-through

45

CHAPTER 11

SERVICE

Serving at tennis is a great art and a highly under-rated one. In response to the direct question, I usually say that there are about fifty different types of service. In actual fact, because one can serve from almost anywhere at the service end, with enormous variations in pace and trajectory, and with numerous methods of applying spin, there are obviously an almost infinite number of services.

From this array a player has to select a range that suits his style and temperament. For example, a fast railroad will invite a violent return and will set up a short, fast rest. By contrast a bobble service will probably induce a slower, spinning reply to the forehand corner. A strong volleyer might pick the former, whereas someone with a suspect backhand might opt for the latter more often.

Some players choose to concentrate on one particular type of service, in the belief that it will be better grooved that way, because chopping and changing will inevitably result in some very loose services. Personally, I take the opposite view: that even if variations in service mar my own serving rhythm, this is more than compensated for by the unsettling effect on my adversary. Furthermore you never know when you may run into someone who just loves receiving that favourite service of yours; or when you may be playing on a court where your speciality isn't very effective. I like to enter a competition with half a dozen front-line services, plus another ten or so once-a-set types. The average club member should try to develop about half that number as a minimum. It will amplify both his versatility and his enjoyment of the game.

As far as technique goes I shall divide serving into four groups, as follows:
1. Those services which carry no spin, in which the object is to achieve perfect length.
2. The spinning services that are designed to keep the ball close to the grille wall, after leaving the penthouse.
3. The spinning services that hug the gallery wall after leaving the penthouse.
4. Other services that have subtleties of spin and flight that induce uncertainty in the opposition.

1. Bobble, boomerang and chandelle.

These three services are all delivered from the centre of the court at about chase last gallery.

Delivering the Bobble Service

(a) For the bobble, the ball is struck from just above knee height in a shallow lob, so that it lands halfway up the penthouse above hazard first gallery. From there it should bumble in an arc nearly to the top of the penthouse and then down again, pitching close to the nick on the grille wall. The skill lies in weighting your pace of stroke against the slope of the penthouse. Length is the primary consideration, but it is also important to try to run the ball up close to the service wall, so that it trundles back down the penthouse and tends to bounce *along* the grille wall, rather than away from it. If your opponent is volleying this service, make sure that it is bobbling, rather than rolling, when it

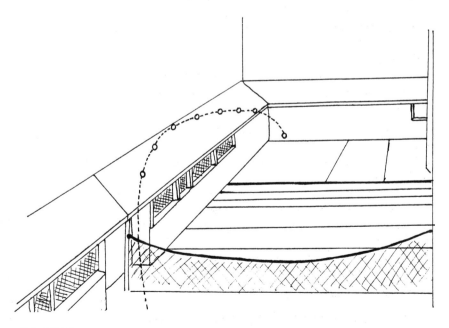

Path of Bobble

47

reaches him, as this will make his task that bit harder. A little topspin may increase the amount of bobble. When delivering the service, take a pace on to your left foot just before you hit the ball, keep your wrist firm and play a long, smooth stroke, rather than a short punch. Use your normal forehand grip.

(b) Much the same technique applies to the boomerang, except that this demands a much firmer stroke that pitches the ball on to the service penthouse between the winning gallery and the grille penthouse. Exactly where it should land depends on the characteristics of that particular penthouse. From there the ball should bounce on to the grille penthouse, then the high back wall, back on to the service penthouse and across the court, near to and parallel with the grille wall. Some players give a little sidespin to the ball as they hit it, in order to take it more to the left off the high back wall. Whenever I try this it results in a lessening of control, so I usually don't bother as touch is all important here. When the length is good, this service is virtually unplayable; when it is bad the ball is a sitter, but it still has the saving grace of being a lifeless ball right at the back of the hazard court. It is one of the fashionable serves of today.

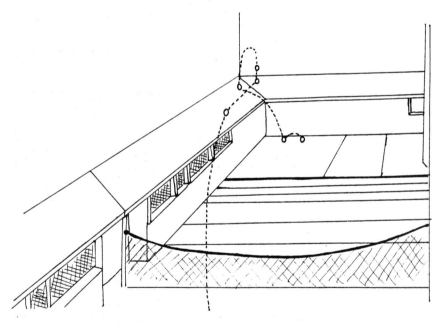

Path of Boomerang

(c) The chandelle is played from the same position, with the same grip and the same pace forwards, but the ball is taken at waist height and struck with a firm, upwards action. It should fly as high as control and available space permit, landing near the intersection between the high side wall (service wall) and the service penthouse, so that it then bounces into the court close to the grille wall. The service that touches the service wall will be similar in length to the one that just misses that wall, so aim for that intersection and let your opponent worry about what it is going to do. If you are confident of striking a good length, this is an ideal service for defending a very short chase, where your opponent is more or less obliged to force for the dedans, because it requires him either to play an overhead volley or else to force a dead ball from very close to the grille wall.

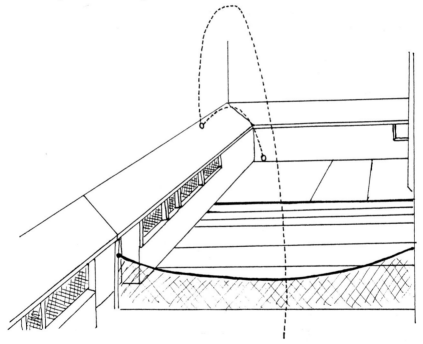

Path of Chandelle

2. Sidewall, high sidewall, drop, giraffe and caterpillar

(a) The sidewall service is one of the staples and has been partially described in the elementary coaching section. Take up a position somewhere near the backhand corner and facing the main wall. Lift the racket above your right shoulder with your elbow well bent. Take a step down the court to the left with your left foot and, simultaneously, lift the

The Sidewall Service

Preparation

Contact

Follow-through

50

ball into the air about shoulder height, slightly to your left and at arm's length away. You should allow it to drop only a few inches before striking it. This is done by coming down on and round the ball, so that you feel as if you are striking the far underside of it. The ball should then travel directly up to the service wall above the service penthouse, where its spin will drag it down sharply on to the penthouse itself. From there it should bounce to the floor, ideally some six feet from the grille wall. Your spin will tend to slow the ball on the floor, and bring it down and towards the tambour off the grille wall. If your opponent volleys it, his return is likely to go to your forehand, whereas if he lets it run to the grille wall he will probably have to play it to your backhand.

As with all other services, your arm and body movements should be relaxed and rhythmical. Finish with your weight on your left leg, with its knee slightly bent.

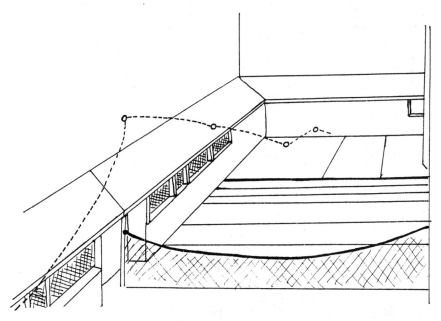

Path of Sidewall Service

(b) The high sidewall service is played in much the same way as the above, except that it is given from the main wall at about chase six and the ball is struck from a few inches lower, along a trajectory that takes it some thirty feet into the air, roof permitting. On its way down it should glance the service wall and then the service penthouse before running, at speed, along the grille wall. It is well worth practising this service

51

The High Sidewall and Drop Services

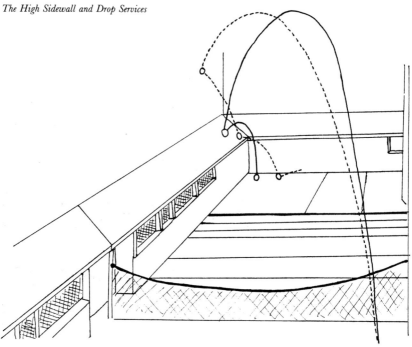

Paths of High Sidewall and Drop Services

52

because, once you have the hang of it, it is great fun to do. However it is one of those types that when it is good it is very, very good, but when it is bad it is a tragedy.

(c) the drop service is exactly the same as the high sidewall except that, instead of striking the service wall first, it drops straight on to the penthouse, whence it should plop on to the floor deep in the receiver's forehand corner and stay there. In practice, when I use these services, I aim for the junction of the service wall and the service penthouse and let the other fellow puzzle over whether he's being dished up a high sidewall or a drop service.

(d) The giraffe is a service that combines a large vertical fall, a favourable spin and the slope of the penthouse, to produce a ball that moves rapidly off the service penthouse, close to and nearly parallel with the grille wall. Normally delivered when standing next to the last gallery, you should begin by facing the centre net, with the racket extended to your right at about chest height. Move your left foot to the left and release the ball in front of your left hip. The racket should then come across the ball from right to left and underneath it, sending it high into the air, spinning clockwise as you see it. Its a tough service to produce, but its also a tough one to take, if you get it right. When you

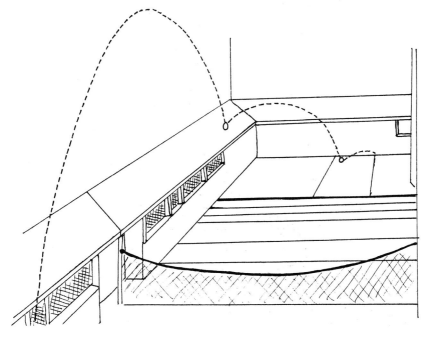

Path of Giraffe

Preparation for Giraffe Service

Contact

Follow-through

54

are experienced, you can meddle with the angle at which it kicks off the penthouse by altering the position of your throw from left to right.

(e) The caterpillar. Now here's a funny service that you don't see too often. Struck overhead like a sliced lawn tennis service, from close to the last gallery, its flight path should be: service penthouse, service wall, back penthouse, high back wall, a leap into the air, down to the floor so close to the grille that it is nearly a fault, and spinning back into the grille wall. Not many courts favour this service as it needs steep, consistent penthouses, but it can be an extra arrow in your quiver, even if you only use it once in each match.

The Caterpillar Service

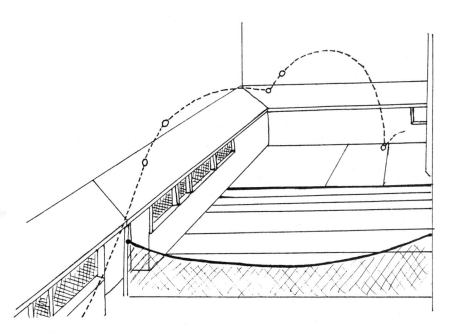

Path of Caterpillar

3. Railroad, classical underarm and drag.

(a) The railroad is recognised as the single most penetrating service in tennis, producing, as it does, more winners than any other type of delivery. It can be a match winner. Strictly speaking, a railroad is any service that runs along the edge of the penthouse. Latterly it has come to refer solely to the overhead American railroad, popularised by Tom Pettitt and perfected by Jay Gould, both American and both former world champions. Oldtimers still term this service 'the American'. Call it what you will, this is how you deliver the damn thing.

Stand at chase three, in line with the backhand corner of the dedans and with your feet pointing towards the second gallery post. Grip the racket with the forehand side uppermost, as if you were going to dong someone over the head with its strings. Then incline your wrist so that the left hand edge of the racket moves away from you, and raise it into position, with your hand by your right shoulder and the racket head dropped over that shoulder. Move your left foot forward a pace and slightly to the left, in the same instant throwing the ball a couple of feet above head height, over your left eye, and far enough forward to make you stretch for it. Keeping the toes of your right foot anchored to the ground, project the racket head in a high arc up, forwards, through and across the ball from right to left, and down past your left shin, finishing behind your back once again. (Take care not to crack yourself one on the shins with this follow-through). Just before impact you should snap your wrist forward, in order to bring the racket face more sharply across the ball. It is the most violent of all the service actions and weight distribution is important. The feeling you should get is that you are trying to put your right shoulder under your left armpit. Do not dally long in this position. If the service is good, it may be returning to you smartly - and probably thirty feet away in the forehand corner.

After it leaves your racket the ball should skip along the bottom third of the penthouse, taking two or three bounces along the way. It should then strike the grille wall a couple of feet above the nick and head back along the side wall, towards the winning gallery. Now there are an awful lot of potential variations and complications, but I do not intend to describe all of them here. It is a difficult service and not everyone is capable of mastering it. If you don't understand or can't get it right, seek the personal advice of a professional.

Preparation for Railroad *Contact*

Follow-through *Completion*

57

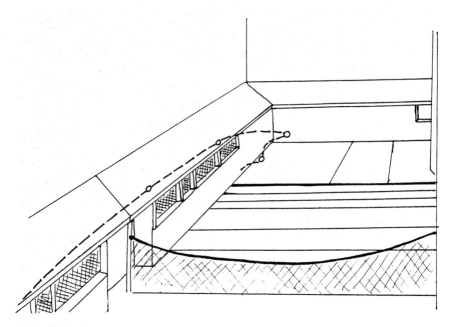

Path of Railroad

(b) The classical underarm twist has the same broad aim as the railroad, in terms of tying up your opponent and it follows roughly the same path along the penthouse, but usually rather slower. Start at chase two, about eight feet from the gallery wall, with your feet pointing straight down the court and your racket dangling vertically in front of you, the racket head close to your ankles and facing towards the tambour. To achieve this angle most people require a slight anti-clockwise adjustment of the wrist. From there, take the racket back past your right leg, cocking your wrist as you do so. The starting position for the swing is about head high, at forty-five degrees behind you. Take a pace forwards and to your left with the left foot and, as you do so, drop the ball down in front of you. Your racket should now drive down along the path it rose, hitting the ball at just above ankle height, with the racket once again almost vertical and facing the tambour. As you strike you should release your wrist, as if trying to hurl your racket underarm into the last gallery. The racket head follows through and should end up somewhere above your head. This upward finish may sometimes cause you problems if it lifts your head up with it. Keep your eyes over the point of impact for as long as you can.

The Classical Underarm Twist

Preparation

Contact

Follow-through

59

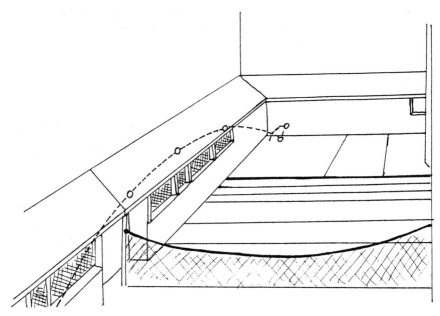

Path of Classical Underarm Twist

(c) The drag is produced by standing at chase two, with your back towards and almost touching the gallery wall. The basic action is the same as a sidewall service action, but it demands great control of line and flight. After leaving your racket, the ball should curve gently in the air and land on the very edge of the penthouse, above hazard first gallery. The spin on the ball is then in conflict with the slope of the penthouse, and the ball should continue along the edge of the penthouse, perhaps taking another bounce or two. When gravity eventually wins the battle, the ball drops to the floor where the residual spin turns it back into the side wall. Once in a blue moon, the ball will leave the penthouse after its first bounce and curve straight into the

The Drag Service

60

winning gallery. This is most upsetting for the receiver because, just as he is preparing to return serve, the ball disappears from view and a point is awarded against him.

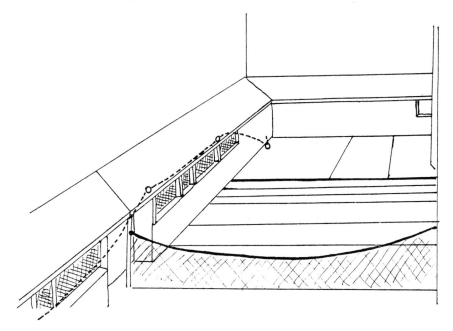

Path of Drag

This is a high-risk service and you must expect to serve a number of faults. That doesn't matter as long as you have a respectable second service to turn to. Far more serious is to project the ball too high up the penthouse so that it bounces more often, losing its length and spin. If this happens, expect to be under the hammer - and hope for a lucky bounce.

4. Underarm variations, piqué and demi-piqué

(a) The classical underarm twist has already been described above. Variations on it should be disguised as far as possible by adopting a similar stance and swing. The differences come about because of the point of contact with the ball and the angle of the racket face. The classic version is hit entirely with sidespin, which is why it leaps back towards the winning gallery off the grille wall. However, if you strike the ball two feet further to your right and two feet further from the ground then the bulk of the rotation imparted is backspin, which will cause the ball

The Cut Underarm Service

to scud along the penthouse and bounce away from the gallery wall when it hits the grille wall - a veritable googly.

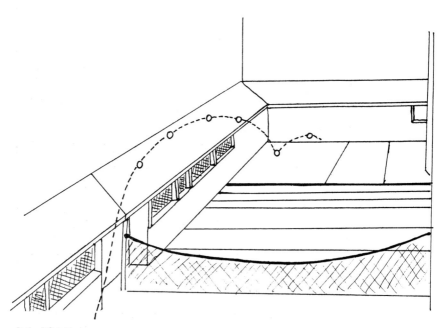

Path of Cut Underarm

By contrast, if you strike the ball much further left than classically, your racket head is no longer moving sideways, but upwards. This gives topspin and makes the ball leap off the penthouse and, if short, it will rear up off the floor at an unwary receiver.

*The Topspin
Underarm Service*

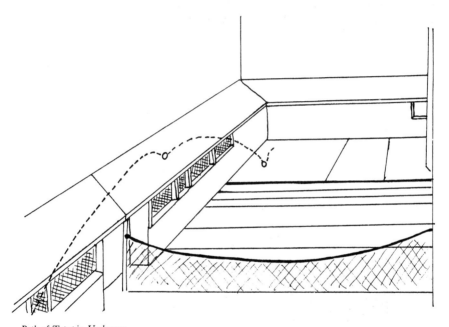

Path of Topspin Underarm

Something else that works for me is throwing the ball a long way forward and having a good hack at it while stretching after it. This could go anywhere, and usually does, but I comfort myself that if *I* don't know where it's going or what it will do then the enemy must be completely baffled.

With a lot of these services I use a shortened grip and really whip my wrist at the ball with everything I've got. The control isn't extra crash hot, but the sight of a ball really fizzing along the roof is often enough to make my opponent lose confidence, drop his racket head and start to think defensively.

The Underarm Hack

(b) The piqué is a service that is thumped with an overhead lawn tennis action, from better than second gallery by the main wall, into the penthouse above hazard the line. From there it deflects off the service wall high into the air, dropping just in play near the grille. This is difficult to return on the volley without hitting across the line of the ball, and causes problems because it moves towards the tambour if it hits the floor first, but dies if it hits the grille wall first.

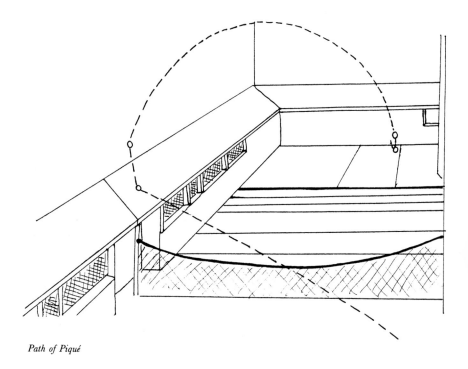

Path of Piqué

The Piqué Service

(c) The demi-piqué is used to unsettle an adversary who favours the volley for returning serve. To deliver it you should stand in the centre of the court on the last gallery line and use a sidewall action, taken just above shoulder height, to knock the ball into the service penthouse above hazard first gallery. It should bounce up to the service wall, and

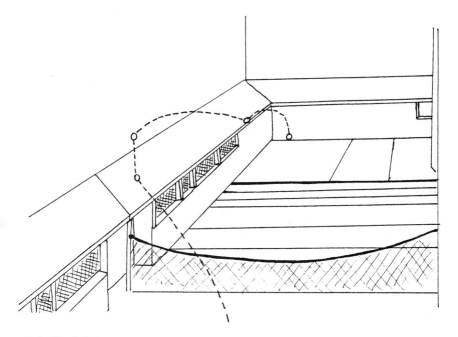

Path of Demi-piqué

off it with enough pace either just to hit or just to miss the penthouse on the way down. This is the factor which will cause uncertainty in the volleyer, especially if the service is used sparingly.

The Demi-piqué Service

CHAPTER 12

RETURN OF SERVE

I go numb at the thought of trying to describe, on paper, how to return all of the above services with all their possible permutations of spin, bounce and length; so what follows is a series of guidelines.

First of all, you have to learn to read the serve. The best method of learning is by accumulating experience, for if you have often received a particular service you are unlikely to be deceived by it. Being capable of delivering the service in question also helps, because then it should hold few terrors for you. Other than that, the only thing you can do is ask for advice and pause each time a service foxes you, in order to work out why you were beaten. Try to think of the ball in terms of its axis of rotation, which alters with each bounce. If, in serving, your opponent's racket moves across his body from left to right as you see it, you should generally expect the ball to break away from you off the grille wall. If the service strikes the service wall at any stage, then expect it to spin towards you off the grille wall. Services that bounce many times on the penthouse discharge much of their spin there and break less severely than the one-bouncers.

An overhit service that rolls off the grille penthouse should cause you no bother. The next easiest one to return is the service which strikes the grille wall before the floor. If your judgment is correct and your footwork snappy, you should be left with a wide choice of options: forcing, cutting or sliding the ball to either side of the court.

Slightly shorter in length is the service that drops in the nick. If you allow it to run its course then you are in trouble, so you have to move in and volley it as it leaves the service penthouse. Try to stay low as you approach the ball and take it round about head height. The lower the ball drops, the more you will be hitting across the line of flight and the more errors will creep in. Keep both the back-swing and the follow-through compact and, particularly, ensure that the latter is not too low, which is a common failing.

Another common weakness, when volleying the return of serve, is that receivers tend to get too close to the ball and end up by swinging at it while their weight is falling away towards the tambour. The way to conquer this is to force yourself to stand a few inches further away from the service penthouse, which will align your feet more correctly. You should also keep your head still on contact, which will prevent over-rotation of the shoulders.

Preparation for the Volleyed Return of Serve

Contact

Follow-through

It is fairly simple to teach yourself to volley the return of serve. Roll a few balls off the service penthouse and apply the technique described above. Once you are happy with the results, make it a little harder for yourself by throwing the ball on to the service wall, so that it bounces down on to the penthouse and then towards you. This makes greater demands upon your footwork. A natural consequence of learning to volley the return of serve is the appreciation of which balls should be dealt with in this fashion and which ones are best left alone until they have bounced.

Services which fall a few feet short of the nick can be returned by applying the approach used for playing shots off the back wall. Assess the spin, move your feet, allow the ball to travel past you and then sweep it away as it comes off the grille wall.

A nick service is a good one because it threatens the receiver who is unwilling to volley. Another good length service is one which has him debating whether the ball has sufficient momentum to give him a shot at it off the back wall; or whether he should step in and take a rising, spinning ball instead. Experience is the only answer, I fear. Some players leap forward to volley this type of service and that has some merit - but it is not a proper substitute for judgment. You should volley as a positive move, rather than out of fear of the alternatives.

The shortest services, other than faults, can be played aggressively off the floor. Maintain a lookout for the effects of spin, keep a firm wrist and attack the ball at the top of its bounce.

In Part One you are advised to await the serve standing close to the grille wall in the centre of the court. More advanced players are recommended to take up a position midway between this point and the near edge of the winning gallery.

Receiving Serve
(Advanced Position)

Special mention must be made of the fast railroad. Should it strike the floor before the grille wall then you can play it like a back wall shot, although you may find yourself within a few inches of the gallery wall as you do so. If it looks like dropping in the nick then you must volley it, using a stroke that is even shorter and crisper than usual. However, if the fast railroad goes according to plan, you may find yourself chasing after a ball that is running at speed close to the gallery wall. Given plenty of room you could slip it cross-court away from the server, or force it, but the best reply is often a boast.

A boast is any shot which is played deliberately into a side wall on your side of, or just beyond, the net. The secret is to remember not to flick it there with the wrist, but to step into your intended direction of stroke. The basic technique used is the same as that for forcing (described later). Take your racket back rather than up, make your hitting stride a large one, deliver the blow from the shoulder rather than the wrist, and stay low at the end. As a return of a fast railroad the boast can be most effective, and you only need a six-inch gap between ball and gallery wall in order to play it.

The Boasted Return of a Fast Railroad

In passing we can note the effect of a boast on the flight of the ball. Coming off the side wall at an acute angle like that, the ball picks up a lot of sidespin. This causes it to swerve in the air, as if trying to return to the same side wall. A bounce on the floor will accentuate that curve, but on striking the back wall the ball will kick the other way.

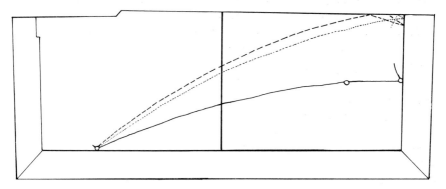

Paths of Boasted Balls

If a boasted ball flies towards a corner it can be very difficult to read. It tends to do the opposite of what you expect, and the rule of thumb that I use is that if the ball strikes the side wall first, it will stay close to that side wall when it comes out of the corner; but if it hits the back wall first, it will pop out into the court.

CHAPTER 13

FORCING

The extent to which you use the force will depend on your physique, temperament and tactics, but everyone needs a force, even if only as the occasional surprise factor. Let's start with the dedans. Of the three winning openings, the dedans is the only one not tucked away in a corner somewhere. Your opponent stands right in front of it and he will gobble up, on the volley, any force at half rat-power. You have three choices: the disguised stroke (which is covered later), the boast off the main wall and the thunderbolt.

The last of these strokes is only played when your opponent puts the ball on the grille wall or grille penthouse. As you are not trying to mask your intentions, you should exaggerate your movements as if to say 'O.K. buddy, you've played a lousy shot and now you're going to pay for it!'

When practising the force, start by hitting a few balls out of your hand. Hold your racket behind you as if you were going to hurl it into the dedans, crouch low, take a large step towards the net and stay low at the end of the swing, finishing on balance so that your back foot remains stationary for a moment. In making this stroke, use full throttle and try to keep the racket head a constant distance from the floor, so that the arc described is a horizontal one. The errors you will make with this arc are usually directional ones and not too serious, whereas a vertical arc which starts high, strikes at the low point and finishes high, will commonly produce mistakes in height of force, which are disastrous. Try also to finish with your racket pointing at the dedans, with an extended arm. I sometimes do this, on the forehand, by catching the throat of the racket in my left hand at the finish and the effect is to smooth out the hitting part of the stroke. When you are satisfied with the shot from the hand, proceed to forcing balls which are rolling off the grille penthouse. Learning the force is a good example of 'practice makes perfect'.

The force for the dedans off the main wall has the advantage that it is harder for the server to defend against and the drawback that, if you miss, he has an easy ball in the middle of the court. You should utilise this tactic, then, only when you rate your chances of success highly. The same items of technique apply, but you should make sure that you do not have to hook the ball across its line of flight. In other words, only play this boasted force when the ball is moving roughly in the right

Preparation for Force

Contact

Follow-through

73

direction anyway. You will also need to sacrifice a little power in order to maximise your control. Some players can force on the backhand as well as the forehand and the boasted force is often a money-spinner for them. Backhand forcing is described in the final part of this book.

Going for the grille with the backhand employs the same stroke as firing for the dedans on that wing; but with the forehand a different stroke is needed. The new factors to be taken into consideration are the height of the net at the main wall and the presence of the tambour. The thunderbolt should only be employed when the ball is well away from the main wall and the centre net is not obscuring the grille. When the ball is within a few feet of the main wall, it should be struck at seventy per cent pace and finely boasted off the main wall, so that it curves round the tambour and into the grille. If you are playing your force from between these two positions, you should aim directly for the bottom half of the grille, at eighty per cent power. Thus if you miss too low the ball will run along the tambour wall, causing the hazard player some difficulty, whereas the boasted force, from this position, which misses the grille will run into the centre of the court and give him an easy shot.

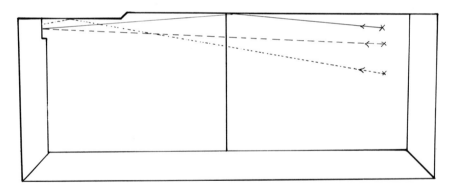

Forcing for the Grille

Often the ability to hit the grille seems to be the difference between winning and losing vital sets, so it is a shot well worth developing. Try playing a few forces out of your hand, both directly for the grille and boasted finely off the main wall. Decide which makes you more comfortable from various positions. Also play a few on the half-volley out of your hand, and then some balls which are rolling off the dedans

74

penthouse. Try to get to the stage where you expect to hit the grille, rather than just hope to hit it.

Moving on to the winning gallery: this is an opening you would normally force for only with a ball wide on the forehand, preferably off the back wall and a long way up the court. Unlike the grille and dedans, the winning gallery has no protection from a volleyer, in singles, so use the stroke over which you have most control. It is prudent to aim for the far, lower edge of the gallery, as a shot too long or too low leaves you better placed than with a ball on the penthouse, or with a hazard chase of second gallery. The exception to this is when the score in a game has advanced to thirty and there is one chase laid against you already. In these circumstances, when you are bound to change ends soon anyway, a hazard chase is no catastrophe, so I advise aiming just to miss the hazard second gallery post.

Whatever force you are attempting, be forthright in your approach to it. Don't waft the ball down to the tambour/grille area in the hope of striking it lucky. Be purposeful and look as if you mean business.

CHAPTER 14

VOLLEYS AND HALF-VOLLEYS

In the old days the volley used to be called the stop, and was used primarily for defensive purposes. Given the choice of a volley or a shot off the back wall, the player of yore would opt for the latter. These days that policy still has merit for the beginner. Even if he is a strong volleyer he must still become acquainted with back wall play, so that he has the choice of both strokes.

Volleying is more prevalent these days and this may have something to do with the sturdier rackets and more forgiving balls now in use. The requirement to defend the openings is still present of course, but, in addition, pressure can be applied with an attacking volley which returns the ball to the other end more rapidly than does any other stroke.

The essentials for volleying are to turn sideways, step down the court to meet the ball, grip the racket firmly, keep the racket head well above the hand even if this means crouching down, extend your arm towards the ball, and use a short, punching stroke that stays on the line of the ball.

Stepping forward gives you a positive attitude to the volley; and pushing the racket out in front of you adds weight and makes it far easier to watch the ball onto the racket. Many players find they have to alter their grips to play the volleys, both forehand and backhand, but I recommend that you try to keep the fingers of the grip in place and simply allow the heel of the hand to slip round so that, in either case, it is behind the handle.

It goes without saying that you should watch the ball carefully while playing any stroke; but when volleying it is doubly important to keep your eyes on the ball. In order to assist your vision, you should attempt to keep your head still as you play your volley and, in turn, this is best promoted by making your positional movements early, so that you are on balance during the stroke.

Half-volleys should be played in the same way as ordinary floor shots but, because you are dropping the racket head more than usual, you must make sure that you keep your head down and that your follow-through is shortish, low and stays on line with the path along which you are hitting.

Players often ask me to define whether hitting along the line means the line of the ball coming towards you or the line of your intended shot. The answer is that it depends on how difficult the ball is. If it is a simple

Forehand Volley Grip   *Forehand Volley*

Backhand Volley Grip   *Backhand Volley*

ball then your racket should follow the line of your stroke, as should your body. The more difficult the ball the more you should swing down the line of its approach, using the racket face to achieve the angle you want. If the ball is very difficult then you are best advised to block it straight back whence it came.

CHAPTER 15

THE TAMBOUR

There are several stages in learning to read the tambour. The complete beginner forgets its existence and is to be found, in a bemused state, by the grille every time the buttress is hit. He now moves to the next stage and over-reacts to the tambour, leaping to the centre of the court each time a ball goes within six feet of it. Eventually he learns that judgment is required, but he always seems to read it the wrong way and then, with growing experience, he starts to get the hang of it.

Just when he thinks he is beginning to understand the tambour, it dawns on him that there are gradations to the abomination. Rather than being a simple question of whether the ball hits the buttress or not, he now finds that the ball can leave the tambour through a range of some sixty degrees, depending on his opponent's position, the spin which has been imparted, and whether the ball glances the main wall and/or the floor before the tambour.

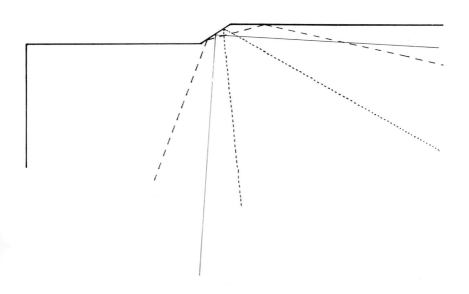

Angles off the Tambour

Shots that strike the main wall before the tambour travel closer to the grille wall than shots that strike the tambour direct. Balls struck from the forehand along the main wall go closer to the grille wall than those hit from the backhand, which sometimes actually set hazard chases. Hitting the floor before the tambour also deflects the shot deeper, towards the grille wall.

Where should you position yourself? (Players at Falkland Palace, Hobart and Oxford should ignore this paragraph). If your opponent plays his shot from close to the main wall, you should make up your mind immediately whether it is going to hit the tambour or not and move into position. Do not attempt to cover both possibilities. If your decision is that the tambour will be hit, your position should be in the centre of the court, about a yard behind the buttress. As a general rule, you should take balls that strike the tambour below head height with your backhand, those about head height with a backhand volley and those higher, on the forehand as they pass you. For the very low balls you will have to dart forward before they bounce a second time, and the very high balls you can let run through to the gallery wall opposite. These will kick slightly off that wall towards the net, but you should still be able to attack them.

The balls you take on the backhand are the most common and to play them you should position yourself facing the tambour, attempting to

Playing a Backhand off the Tambour

take the ball opposite your front foot. Get down low, stay low and play a short, flat stroke at the ball. The safe direction to return shot is back up the main wall, as this is less across the line; but, if you are confident, then a gentle shot to the other side will curl naturally into the corner.

A greater problem is how to cope with balls heading for the tambour from your opponent's backhand. There are four distinct possibilities and, because the ball is travelling cross-court, there are no reference points to guide you and it is much harder to judge what it will do.

Firstly, the ball may miss the tambour and finish up under the grille.

The second possibility is that the ball will hit the tambour's angled face directly. If this happens then the ball will lose a lot of pace and head in the general direction of the winning gallery.

Thirdly, the ball may glance off the main wall before hitting the buttress. This one will be moving much faster, because each of these two deflections are fine ones, and the final direction will be towards the receiver's forehand corner.

Finally, the ball may hit the main wall a little nearer the net and subsequently miss the tambour. It will then move along a path nearly parallel to the first of the options described above.

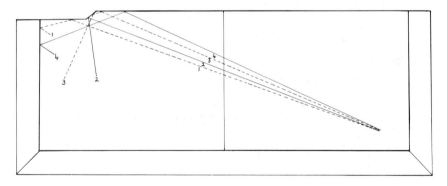

Angles Around the Tambour

How do you deal with these balls? Well, if the ball is moving slowly, you should think positively, determine quickly which of the four possibilities this is, and either intercept the ball early or commit yourself to a position without compromise, so that you are either well-placed or hopelessly stranded.

81

More frequently you will have to cope with a fast-moving shot in this area. Personally I advocate making a quick decision and, on that basis, covering either shots 1 and 2 in the diagram or else shots 3 and 4. If you cover 2 and the ball misses the edge of the tambour, you should be able to scramble back for 1; and if you set yourself for 3 and the ball hits the main wall only, then 4 should not be too difficult. If your opponent's shot is a quick one, then I suggest you don't try to cover all the options, as you could end up covering none of them to any good effect.

As for technique when taking these nasty balls off the tambour, you should acknowledge their difficulty and play accordingly. You are obliged to hit across the line of the ball in terms of direction, but at least try to keep your entire swing at the height at which you are taking the ball. Don't lift your head as you play the stroke and make sure that your swing is compact.

CHAPTER 16

LEFT-HANDERS

At most games left-handed players usually start with a slight advantage. Some folks believe that, as a minority group, they have to be slightly tougher to survive and this gives them an edge over their right-handed peers. This may or may not be valid, but what is indisputable is that the contrariness of a southpaw tends to upset the pattern of his opponent's game. How many club cricketers would rather the unknown bowler taking the new ball was not a leftie? How many Australian Rules footballers have got away from their man because they circled clockwise on the left foot after marking?

At tennis, I believe the left-hander is penalised by the asymmetry of the court rather more than he benefits from it. In other words, any advantage he gains on service and in defence of the tambour is outweighed by the requirement that he returns the vast majority of services on the backhand. This is not a monumental disadvantage and can be compensated for by the adoption of strokes and tactics that accentuate the left-handedness.

Most players can apply more cut and can hit harder on the forehand than on the backhand. A right-hander will therefore normally return serve aggressively, with a relatively high risk of error, because he knows that if a long rest gets going, being at the hazard end, he is likely to get the worst of it. If you are cack-handed (and I shall assume this for the remainder of the section) then you should temper your aggression and go for a more controlled, semi-attacking shot, with no errors. Consider the position of the server. He expects an attacking return of serve, and is normally content simply to retrieve this first shot and to shovel the ball back somewhere towards the tambour. Against most players this is sound strategy, for the average backhand has limited attacking power and the server feels he is tilting the balance of the rest in his favour. But against you he has a problem: if he makes his usual defensive push towards the tambour then he is playing to your strength (and even if your backhand is more consistent, it won't appear to be as menacing as your forehand). If he switches his attack to your backhand he will almost certainly make many more mistakes than usual, because he is altering his natural game.

To sum up: if you are receiving serve make your first return a solid one, at eighty per cent pace and cut. Then, if you are rallying with your opponent, exaggerate the danger of your forehand, so that he fears to aim for the grille/tambour region.

Left-handers have an advantage when playing balls off the tambour, not only because of the forehand strength, but also because they are more capable of reaching behind themselves to flick back shots that have touched the main wall before the buttress.

The general technique for strokes is the same as for right-handers, except that you should develop the habit of taking the ball slightly further forward on the forehand and marginally further back on the backhand. This is because your tactics should be to hit nearly all forehands cross-court and most backhands along the side walls.

Differences arise on service and return of serve. A left-handed railroad can be a devastating weapon, and there are many other services which you can employ that are not only very effective, but also cause accentuated uncertainty in your opponent because he is far less likely to have come across those services before.

I shall not attempt to describe all of the left-handed services in detail. In general I would advise you to avoid backhand services if you are a leftie, because what you will achieve is a right-handed service that has been watered down. Have a go at all the right-handed service actions, applying as much spin as possible. As this spin is in reverse, you should

The Left-hander's Railroad (Steve Ronaldson)

aim the balls struck with underarm actions for the service wall above the service penthouse, and keep the balls spun with sidewall actions running along the penthouse.

The left-handers railroad can be delivered from nearly anywhere at the service end, but usually it is from about chase three, a few feet from the side penthouse. You should start by facing this penthouse, with your racket hand a foot above your left shoulder and the racket head behind your left shoulder blade, face vertical. From this position you take a step forward and to your right with your right foot, at the same time tossing the ball, in the same direction, to a height two feet above your head and within comfortable reach of your racket. You then strike at the ball, attempting to hit it on the upward part of your swing, bringing the racket face across the upper left hand side of the ball, as you look at it, and finishing the stroke with your left hand near your right pocket. This service should bounce two or three times on the penthouse and leap off the grille wall towards the winning gallery.

If I had been born the wrong way round I would spend a lot of time practising the drag. The advantage you have here is that you can strike this service at a foot from the penthouse, whereas a right-hander is

The Left-hander's Drag (Steve Ronaldson)

obliged to hit the ball from at least four feet away, if he is to avoid tying himself up in knots. You should start by standing on chase two, about three feet from the side penthouse and facing the last gallery. Throw the ball in front of your left leg and strike it at knee height, coming across and under the ball, with a stroke that starts with the racket face open behind your left shoulder and finishes with the racket pointing towards the main wall at head height. The swing should be fast yet the ball should move only slowly, the stroke having imparted spin, rather than pace. Control is all-important, and the service should climb only just high enough to get onto the bottom foot of the penthouse. Once there, it should scud along this line for some three or so bounces, still spinning like a top, before dropping to the floor and wreaking havoc with your opponent's nerves.

I have already advised you to return serve more conservatively than a right-handed player. There are a couple of exceptions to this, with which you may care to experiment. One is to step inside short services and take them on your forehand. By doing this you are hitting across the line of the ball, and thus you should adopt this ploy only if you are confident of reading the service correctly. Play a cut stroke, directed short and on line with the forehand corner of the dedans; you will find

'Stepping Inside' to Return Serve (Steve Ronaldson)

that the ball curls wickedly into the corner of the court, both in the air and off the floor. It causes the server problems not only because it is a good stroke, but also because it is an unusual one.

The other trick comes when receiving a very good serve that is running parallel with and very close to the grille wall, such as a boomerang. The right-hander has a choice of lobbing, or boasting the ball off the side wall above the penthouse. The latter finishes up as an easy ball in the forehand corner with the tambour begging to be attacked, so neither option is very good. A left-hander can nip around the other side of the ball and play his forehand boast into the main wall. This is a superior boast in that it can be struck low, as there is no penthouse to clear, and because the server has to take a low, spinning ball in his backhand corner.

Given a little more room, you can disguise this cross-court boast with a straight force to the forehand corner of the dedans, although you would normally only use this deception when striking balls that roll off the grille penthouse or balls that hit the grille wall before the floor.

When attacking very short chases, most right-handers will try to force very aggressively for the dedans on the return of serve. Canny left-handers frequently adopt a different course of action. Unless the service is very easy and invites a force, they return serve with a high lob designed to land at chase 2 on the server's backhand. This shot threatens to bounce into the dedans, and few servers are capable of doing more than prodding the ball tentatively towards the tambour. Then, in theory at least, the southpaw steps in and belts the ball into the dedans with his forehand.

CHAPTER 17

GENERAL TACTICS

The vast majority of tennis players score better from the service end than from the hazard end. Sometimes this is not very obvious to the onlooker, as for ten or fifteen minutes the combatants may have mixed success at each end. Then, all of a sudden, there will be a little burst of dominance by one of the players. It may last for only six or seven points, but it often decides the outcome of that set and it is almost always the server who achieves this run of points. Frequently the server does not play any better: he just seems to have become luckier, and that's the secret of it - there is more good fortune to be had when on the service side. Not only are there more nicks, edges and corners to be found at the hazard end, but you can aim for the grille, score with a winning shot off the tambour instead and no-one will ever know that you failed to strike your intended target.

In a nut-shell, this then is your strategy: spend as much time as possible at the service end and direct most of your shots towards the grille and tambour.

Developing this theme, you have to find ways of setting chases to gain the service, and ways to avoid conceding them so that you can remain serving. There are three common methods of setting chases: by aiming for the side galleries; by forcing underneath the dedans; and by playing classic floor shots to the corners. The first two yield frequent chases of poor quality and the last produces good chases, but less often.

The techniques for these strokes have already been described, but not the exact flight paths. Personally, I don't care much for the policy of chipping for the galleries, as it is rather tedious, but when the need arises I aim for the second gallery post and low rather than high.

The low force should be directed on a line such that, if your opponent chases after it, he has to play his stroke at a ball which is clinging to one of the side walls. Usually, this entails aiming your force underneath the corners of the dedans, but clearly it depends on your own position and what sidespin, if any, you impart.

The most popular way of obtaining a chase is the conventional cutting of the ball to a length and this is the one that deserves the most attention. If you are playing this stroke from the floor, you will find it difficult to control your length and I recommend that you block the ball firmly, so that it bounces in the nick or just before it, and as near the corners as possible. As long as your aim is fairly true, your opponent will have to read the corner correctly and then dig out a low, fast ball after it has hit the dedans wall.

If the stroke you are playing is off the grille wall, you should be able to control the length and line far better. Therefore you should aim these shots so that they hit the floor at chase six and the side wall at chase four. Your opponent can cut many of these shots off before they reach the dedans wall, but he will find it difficult to counter-attack, and this use of the side walls ensures that he runs the maximum width of the court from his central position.

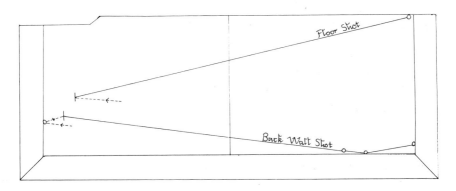

Ideal Lengths for Strokes

As for avoiding chases when you are at the service end, this will depend on your opponent's game. If he is inclined to aim for the galleries, then you should keep your services close to the gallery wall and short, rather than long. During the rests you should try not to over-hit strokes for the grille, as it is easier to tickle balls into the galleries from off the back wall than from off the floor.

If the receiver is the forcing type, your best counter is to move up the court from your normal position at about chase two to nearer chase four, whenever you see him winding up for a big smack. This may seem like advising you to walk into trouble but, in fact, it gives you a good positive attitude to volleying, if that turns out to be necessary, and you will also be better placed to chase after the ball that cannons off the dedans wall and careers up the court.

Should your opponent prove to be a floor game specialist, then you should have two main tactical threads running through your overall game-plan. You should raise the pace of the game so that he loses the control that is so vital to his strategy; and you should concentrate on serving tightly and defensively, so that, unless he sacrifices some control in favour of deception, he can play his cut stroke to only one of the two corners at your end. For example, a slow railroad invites a cross-court cut and a good sidewall service restricts your opponent's cut shot to your backhand corner. Thus limited, the receiver's effectiveness is reduced by the predictability of his strokes.

CHAPTER 18

DOUBLES PLAY

Singles at tennis is an attacking game. The court is long and wide, the balls are hard, move fast and take spin, and there are plenty of angles to be exploited. With such a good variety of attacking possibilities, the aggressive player will normally defeat a safety-first competitor of similar talent and experience.

By contrast doubles, or the four-handed game as it used to be known, is essentially defensive. This is not to say that there is no worthwhile form of attack in doubles, because the pace is often faster than in singles, but rather that such bombardment is designed to force mistakes rather than to produce clean winners. With a man in each corner and most openings well protected, it is hard to find the gaps in the opposition consistently. Consequently, an experienced pair will try to probe weaknesses in its foe, while keeping its own unforced errors to a minimum.

The rules for doubles are the same as for singles except for some extra regulations governing service and return of serve. At the beginning of a set, the serving team must nominate one of its pair who will serve the first game and all the odd games of that set, whenever they are at the service end. His partner will deliver service on all the even games. The receiving team must then elect who will receive serve and give service in the odd games, and his partner will be responsible in the even games. The appointed receiver must always return the serve unless the ball served drops between the centre line and the fault line, in which case either he or his partner may play the ball. Service and receipt of serve apart, there are no restrictions about which player has to strike any particular ball.

The rests in doubles tend to be longer than in singles, which means that the angles around the tambour come more into play. In turn this makes the service end even more attractive than in singles and chases more important. With two players covering the service end it is less easy to lay a chase on the floor and gallery chases are attempted more frequently.

Normally, one of the serving pair defends the galleries to prevent chases, while his partner plays the majority of returns elsewhere on the court. If the ball is in the receiver's forehand corner then it is unlikely to be aimed successfully for the galleries, and so the player defending them will often drop back to assist his partner in dealing with floor shots and

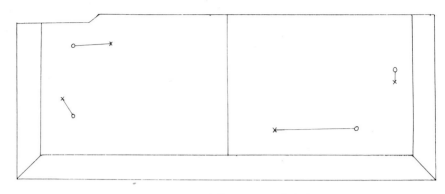

o = Position when ball is in opposite forehand corner
x = Position when ball is in opposite backhand corner

Positioning in Doubles

forces. The nearer the ball is to the main wall at the hazard end, the more exposed the galleries become and the further this player will need to advance in order to defend them.

At the hazard end the service receiver, having returned serve, should assume that every ball heading towards the grille corner is going to strike the tambour and he should cover that shot. His partner, meantime, assumes that every ball will miss the tambour, so that between the two of them they attend to both possibilities.

The main function of this last player is to defend the grille. If the ball is about to be played by one of his opponents from the server's forehand corner, he should station himself on the fault line some four or five feet behind the tambour (see diagram) with his racket held ready for a backhand volley. However, if the ball is in the server's backhand corner, he will find it difficult to protect the grille from a shot that just misses the tambour, so he should move directly forward to the service line and play his volleys from there. If the ball is struck into the main wall next to or in front of him, he should allow it to pass and let his partner deal with it.

The best doubles players are usually strong volleyers and steady ground stroke players who make few unforced errors.

PART THREE

CHAPTER 19

OXFORD

Peter Dawes glanced uneasily at me over the top of the car that he had just parked outside the Oxford University Tennis Club. After completing his training at Lords, Peter had been enticed to Oxford in 1965 to become the first full-time professional there for many years. Oxford was, and remains, a vital court in British tennis as it is one of the nurseries of the game, along with Canford and Cambridge. Peter was popular and successful in his aim to build up court usage both by students and by local inhabitants. After six years of hard work he had been given permission to train an assistant, and the Young Professionals Fund had agreed to subsidise this training.

Finding an assistant had not, however, proved easy and the only applicant, following his initial advertisement, had been a fifteen-year-old boy with only one lung and little experience of ball games. I was the second candidate, four weeks later and Peter wasn't sure that I was much of an improvement on the first. I was twenty-one, long-haired, unshaven and had just walked from the building site where I was employed as a chain-boy, holding metre-rules while engineers peered at me through their theodolites and took readings.

If Peter wasn't too sure about me then the feeling was mutual. I had left the University of Kent at Canterbury a couple of months earlier with a B.Sc (fail) to my name and the consequently-reinforced intention of becoming a lawn tennis professional. After a holiday in South Africa and a few lawn tennis tournaments it became apparent that it was time to do some work, and it gradually dawned on me that September was no time to set oneself up as a lawn tennis coach in Britain. I had just found myself this awful job on the building site when a friend pointed out the advertisement that Oxford University Tennis Club required an assistant. Twelve years later that friend, Alan Oliver, successfully applied for the same job himself. I knew enough to recognise that this meant real tennis, but because it offered the chance to learn to string rackets and because anything was better than standing around a freezing construction site in winter, clutching a rule and counting down the minutes to the next tea-break, I decided to give it a go anyway.

Peter Dawes was a famous sportsman! I had often read about him in the newspaper reports of real tennis and, even though I couldn't tell a hazard chase from a railroad service, this guy was obviously pretty good at it. It was hard to believe, mind you, just looking at him: five foot four, nine stone and walking with a decided limp.

Peter Dawes

In those days the entrance to the Oxford court was at the hazard end, and to reach the changing rooms and professional's shop, one had to walk along the poorly-lit stone corridor behind the galleries and up a treacherous spiral staircase at the end. Peter had acquired his limp, as well as a dislocated shoulder, by falling down those stairs. It was all rather gloomy and mediaeval, but the students liked it and the place definitely had character.

Within an hour I had been accepted for the job, had persuaded the foreman at the building site to release me immediately, and had returned to Merton Street to start life as a real tennis professional. My first task was to strip the covers off an old set of balls. I can't remember how the rest of the day went, but I returned home happy.

Peter was a great bloke to work with. He was even-tempered and generous and gave me plenty of time to settle in. He even allowed me to do a little free-lance lawn tennis coaching to supplement the meagre £8 per week that constituted my wages. Above all, he gave me a good start by teaching me the fundamentals of how to play the game and how to behave as a club professional.

Not everything went smoothly. Try as he might, he could not teach me the habit of calling all the club members 'Sir'. I was prepared to address them as 'Mr .....', but no more. Now, barely a dozen years later, I am considered old-fashioned because I seldom use Christian names.

The next problem was the tea revolution. Peter had been trained at Lords, and at Lords the kettle is boiled just before the hour, every hour, for the tea to be made. This habit of drinking tea all the time had spread to every court in the country except Cambridge, where Brian Church used to drink a measure of whisky on the hour. One day Lesley Lee, who was my fiancée, was visiting us at the OUTC and boiled the kettle. She had been shopping, and was laden with groceries, including coffee. 'Want a cup of coffee?' I offered Peter - and threw him into complete confusion. 'Well ..er..why..what about ... I suppose... tea....I...er..yes...yes, why not? I'd love a cup of coffee'. So he got one, and he enjoyed it, but it still didn't feel right to him. He still felt that he was betraying his profession.

Peter had an uncomplicated way of teaching tennis, developed from trying to impart as much knowledge as possible, as simply as possible, to impoverished students who couldn't afford many lessons. I was a fairly slow learner and it took me hours of practice to produce something like the shots he was demanding. Some things came more easily than others. Having spent several days trying to get my awkward limbs to produce a natural-looking sidewall service Peter decided to move on to the railroad. Now Peter's railroad has always been something of a joke and his first three demonstration services whistled harmlessly into the last gallery. When he invited me to have a go I immediately produced a better railroad than he had ever done. Even at Oxford, where the penthouse is six inches lower than normal, height is important for the railroad service.

My employment had started on 14th September 1971 and a couple of months later Lesley and I got married - not that anybody else knew about it, except the two ceremony witnesses. At the time I was considered, quite justifiably, by Les' parents to be a bad influence on her and particularly on her career at Kent University, where she had just entered her final year. So we were married in secret. Three days later I set off for a fortnight's honeymoon in East Africa, but with my father and not with my new bride. It was a pre-arranged trip to Tanzania, where Dad had worked for fifteen years, in order to celebrate the tenth anniversary of that country's independence. We had a great time revisiting old friends and places; but he didn't find out then that he had a daughter-in-law. That came later.

On match days Peter's wife, Vivian, used to provide the lunches and one day she tried to poison us all with a particularly nasty mincemeat tart that had us running to the toilet for days on end. Peter had to take a couple of days off work and when he returned he had picked up a heavy cold to compound his problems. Murphy's Law prevailed and that day the drains decided to get blocked. Peter rolled up his sleeves and leapt into action. An enduring memory of that era is of looking out of the window at Peter Dawes trying to unblock those drains. Without a sense of smell to tell him what my nose was telling me, he was reaching down and ladling out armfuls of sewage while under the impression that it was dead leaves and mud.

Peter never quite made it as a top tennis player. In his early years there was almost no opportunity for match play and he lacked real weight of shot. Later on, when the accidents struck, his speed and agility disappeared. Falling downstairs, tripping over seat belts, slipping on icy patches - you name it, he managed it, and it was always his legs that suffered. In the eight or so months that we shared together Peter was hardly ever fit.

Sadly for me, it was all over too soon and the Dawes had moved to Seacourt, leaving me holding the baby at Oxford. Life wasn't too difficult in the summer, but when the Michaelmas term rolled around it became very hectic. Because of the high percentage of student usage Oxford was, and is, a poor club and even as senior professional my wages were only £16 per week, with negligible coaching fees on top. Thus the bulk of my income came from running a sports shop, and most of my time was spent stringing squash rackets - up to a dozen a day.

As with most sports, the University fixture list is dominated by the Blues match which, in tennis, is held in March. Oxford had beaten Cambridge in 1972 for the first time in many a long year, which was an appropriate farewell for Peter Dawes, but unfortunately the four leading players had left that summer and I had to build a team from scratch. By contrast, Cambridge were able to field the same two-man Blues team from the previous year.

There were two bright spots on my horizon. One was Jonny Leslie, whom I knew from my lawn tennis days, and who was in his final year at Oxford. He had already won his colours at rackets, squash, lawn tennis and rugby fives and I knew he would be tempted by the possibility of a record fifth Blue. The other was news that the Winchester rackets pair of Alan Lovell and Peter Seabrook were both coming up to Oxford.

Jonny had a problem: he was captain of squash, with the Varsity match to be played in December and he also had to do some work. We agreed that he should take up the game in the Hilary term, go like hell at it for six weeks - and hope that this would be sufficient.

Lovell and Seabrook proved even more troublesome. They were concentrating on winning Blues at rackets and lawn tennis, and had no intention of learning a new game, so my initial entreaties were fruitless. However, I did run the fastest racket repair service in town and, once a week, they would be subjected to half an hour of cajoling on the matter, while I effected their repairs. One day the court was empty when they came in, so I gave them a couple of rackets and bullied them on to the court. When I had finished the repairs I sneaked into the dedans to watch them. They looked at ease and at home already, and I knew then that my problems for the University team were over. The only flaw in the exhibition they were giving came when Alan Lovell, playing at the hazard end, turned on the ball as it came off the grille wall and hammered it straight at the winning gallery. 'Oh dear.' he said, scratching his head, 'No wall!!'

Alan Lovell and Peter Seabrook were roughly similar in terms of potential, but Alan was by far the more assiduous student of the game. That first introduction came on a Wednesday. On the following Saturday he played (and won) at No. 5 in the first team, and three weeks later he was playing first string, a place he held for the rest of his university career. Peter's progress was steady but less meteoric and, although he played in the first team that season, he was destined to wait another year before winning his Blue in the two-man team.

A team comprising Lovell and Leslie was duly selected to meet Willcocks and Colquhoun of Cambridge. The first match was the doubles, and most thrilling it was too. Oxford won the first set from 1-5 down, lost the second from 5-2 up and won the third from 3-5 down,

O.U.T.C. 1973. Left to Right: Alan Lovell, Chris Sutton-Mattocks, Chris Ronaldson, Tonny Leslie, Brian Witherden, Peter Seabrook.

eventually winning 6-5, 5-6, 6-5, 6-3. On the second day Alan fought back bravely from two sets down to John Willcocks and only lost in the fifth set; and Jonny won the match for us by beating Duncan Colquhoun in straight sets.

Oxford also beat Cambridge in the Dinner Match that year. The Dinner Match was played in those days between the respective numbers three, four and five on either side and, by tradition, the losers paid for the night out afterwards. Since the advent of the four-man Blues team, the Dinner Match has been abandoned. Our team of Brian Witherden, Chris Sutton-Mattocks and Peter Seabrook won the match for us, and we all had a good night at the Café Royal. For some reason it was also tradition that Oxford arranged the venue, and in that year (and maybe in all the others) not only did Oxford book the Café Royal but also Joe's Fish Bar in Edgware; so that the outcome of the Dinner match not only measured our success but also determined the quality of the entertainment afterwards.

That period was also memorable for me because it was on 1st January 1973 that Michael Floyd Dean became my first assistant. These days Mick is a respectable schoolmaster, married, kids and all that. By and large he has little to do with those who knew him in his late 'teens and early twenties - and for good reason: they uniformly embarrass him with recollections of his former unsavoury habits. As the last relic of those dark years I regard it as my personal duty to ensure that Mick never becomes too smug.

Actually, by 1973 the tide was already turning and Mick's lurid life-style was receding along with his hair-line. His lunch still consisted of a peanut-butter sandwich and two packets of ginger-nut biscuits, and he still insisted on wearing all his clothes in rotation without ever washing them, but he had given up swearing (mostly) and no longer drank such copious quantities of ale each evening.

I had first met Mick on the junior lawn tennis circuit where we had played several close matches. Although we went to separate universities we always kept in touch, usually by wearing our sports socks for weeks on end and then posting them to each other for approval. I once sent Mick some fudge that I had made with all the usual ingredients, plus a few extra - marmalade, peanut butter, cayenne pepper, mustard, tomato sauce, ginger powder etc. etc. It took him two months to finish, at a piece a day, but he did it.

Truth to tell, I was nowhere near senior enough to have an assistant and Mick only stayed with me for three months before moving to Lords for

101

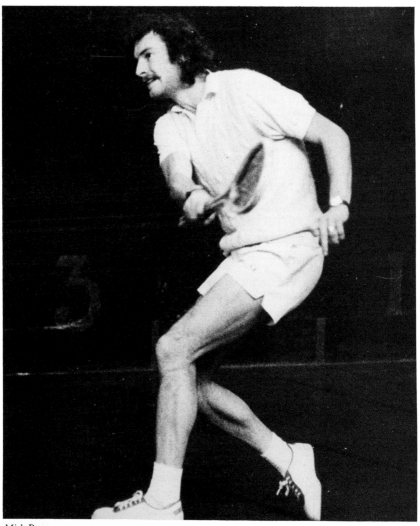

Mick Dean

a spell. In those three months I tried to share my scant knowledge with him and we used to practise conscientiously, both separately and together.

Individual practice is essential for any aspiring player, to be mixed in with tuition, training, games and competition. The best way to begin moulding a stroke is to strike the ball from out of your hand. This gives you as much time as you need to prepare yourself, and allows you to concentrate on particular aspects of the stroke without being under any pressure to time the ball. For example, you may wish to give yourself a new starting-point for the racket on a particular stroke; and you don't have to release the ball until you are satisfied that you have it right. You can then repeat the stroke until the starting-point feels natural.

The next method involves rolling balls off the side penthouse and grooving the cut stroke. This requires a little timing, but not much because the ball is moving so slowly. I spent hours and hours doing this, especially on the forehand, so that I would be in a position to punish severely anyone who served too short at me.

Competence at putting away the very easy ball is important. It is terribly frustrating to play a tactically sound rest that induces your opponent to over-hit in desperation and then, with the court at your mercy, either to muff the shot completely or else to play it so ineffectually that you lose all the hard-earned advantage that you had gained. The best training for this is to stand at the back of the court and biff balls with an overhead action into the back penthouse at your end, so that they rise in a high arc and drop at around chase five or six (or equivalent at the hazard end). Then take the ball at the top of its bounce and try to bury it. You will find it very important to keep a firm wrist and to concentrate on your footwork.

The last of the basic practice exercises is patting - so called because you pat the ball down into the floor and back wall on the forehand and then play the ball backhanded over the net. This is an excellent routine for improving footwork and control of back wall strokes. You should start at about chase one and two, and pat the ball down on to the floor so that it would bounce next at about chase worse than two after the back wall, should you leave it. There should be four paces taken during this exercise: the first backwards as you pat the ball and the other three forwards as you play your stroke. In practice, because of the limited time available you take more of a skip-step than three distinct paces. Try to lay the face of the racket open and keep the ball as short as possible at the other end of the court - any mug can hit the ball hard: control should come first.

Practice from both ends of the court. Naturally, if it is the forehand that needs attention, you have to pat the ball down with a backhand stroke.

The Oxford court was effectively run in those days by Vice-Admiral Sir Peter Gretton who, as Hon. Treasurer, had the unenviable task of trying to sort out the Club's pitiful finances. He used to have a ship's inspection of the premises once a week, which always occasioned some frantic last-minute clearing away, and even so we seldom came up to scratch. Mind you, Sir Peter's bark was much worse than his bite and we never actually had to walk the plank, but without him the Club would not have functioned at all.

It was fun being the pro at Oxford, and very rewarding to give lessons to the young and gifted. The intellectual atmosphere of the place was invigorating and there were heaps of interesting characters. Outstanding among these was one Patrick Traill. Patrick took up tennis before I did and was still at Oxford when I left. He would describe himself as completely unco-ordinated and reports of his early attempts at the game confirmed this. However, by dint of hard work he developed a very fine and correct stroke, and regularly played for the Unicorns, which is the University second team.

Patrick was a mathematician at Merton College and was quite mad, in a brilliant sort of way. His first major contribution to tennis was the Traillroad, which was a sort of underarm twist delivered while standing on the penthouse at the service end. It wasn't obligatory to be inebriated to deliver this service, but Patrick very often was. He and his friends used to play extraordinary handicap games in which you were penalised, on winning a game, by having to consume a certain amount of alcohol, and in which bisques were awarded for misdemeanours such as swearing or belching. The recipient of a bisque had to eat a dry biscuit when he claimed his bisque and I well recall Patrick being awarded a bisque when he stood at match-point, because of some transgression by his opponent, but being unable to take it because his stomach was too insecure to accept another biscuit. These matches were invariably accompanied by stentorian operatic singing from the dedans spectators and the whole scene was quite beyond me.

Patrick's second gift to the game was an ingenious system for recording on paper the scores and details of a match. Although seldom used it is far superior to any other recording system around and, if it takes the operator a few minutes to get acquainted with it, the principle is quite simple and the quantity of information stored for post-match analysis is prolific.

Patrick achieved a first in his finals and, so the story goes, found time to write some poetry on his examination papers. He used to infuriate his bank because of his habit of writing cheques in pounds and florens (sic) rather than in pounds and pence, and he used to infuriate his peers because he insisted on counting in dozenry instead of the conventional decimal system. Dozenry, for the uninitiated, involves counting: one two three four five six seven eight nine bip bop ten eleven twelve

104

thirteen fourteen fifteen sixteen seventeen eighteen nineteen bipteen bopteen twenty twenty-one .....twenty-nine twenty-bip twenty-bop thirty etc. etc. Now this sort of stuff is OK for a bit of fun, but when it invades normal life it can get on top of you. A simple tennis score of 40-15 suddenly becomes 34-13, an outside temperature of seventy degrees is described as fifty-bip degrees, and Patrick would announce that he was born in the year 1166.

How he found time for studying was a mystery to us at the court, for what time he didn't spend playing tennis he seemed to spend in the pro shop. Typically he would wander around the room for hours on end mouthing, at a furious pace, a cross between a murmur, a mutter and a hum. As if this wasn't bad enough, he would always pick up a loose ball and throw it from hand to hand as he lurched about, and his hand-eye co-ordination was such that every twenty seconds or so he would drop the ball, grunt in surprise, and then scrabble about under some chair for it. For us tennis professionals, merely mortal, it was a performance that took some getting used to.

Patrick once asked me to give him a lesson on volleying. He rightly felt that he was good off the penthouse, solid off the back wall and reasonable off the floor, but that too many balls would sail past him unchallenged into the dedans. He wrongly felt that he could do something about this. Although my scepticism was clear he insisted on giving it a bash. The very first ball I hit to him came off the edge of the frame of his racket and smashed his glasses. Wallop - end of lesson on volleying. Patrick accepted defeat and, after clearing up the broken glass, he suggested that perhaps we might fill the hour by playing a game. This also met with professional scepticism because, without his glasses, Patrick was as blind as a bat. Having taken the balls to serve, I decided to let him have the easiest possible service - a short, slow bobble, so I moved right up to the second gallery to deliver it. Patrick showed no sign of recognition that I had struck the ball. He just blinked at me. The ball rolled slowly round the penthouse towards him, but he still appeared oblivious. At the last possible moment he must have seen, heard or smelt the ball because he suddenly took an almighty swing at it, hitting it on the wood just above his thumb. In panic I realised that somehow he had returned the ball and it was going over my head in a slow lob. Back-pedalling smartly from the second gallery, I lunged overhead at the ball and struck it firmly and squarely into the pit of his stomach. Wallop - end of game. Even for a poetic mathematician it wasn't a very productive hour. He hadn't learned to volley and he hadn't had a game. He had hit two balls on the wood of his racket, smashed his glasses, and taken an almighty blow to the belly.

The hot news in the world of tennis at that time was that a brand new court was being built, for the first time in over half a century, in Melbourne, Australia. Late in 1972 I wrote to the Tennis & Rackets Association, the sport's governing body in Britain, asking for details. I was informed that the Royal Melbourne Tennis Club was selling its property in the centre of Melbourne, moving to a nearby suburb, building two new courts, and looking for a professional. It was exciting and I wanted to be part of it.

Despite all Oxford's charms - and there are many - it was not the place to develop into a front-line professional. The main problems were the dependency on the shop for a living and all the work that that entailed, and the nature of the Oxford court itself. All courts are different but Oxford is probably more different than any of them - save Falkland Palace, which is really a jeu quarré court, rather than jeu à dedans. Oxford is the smallest court, has the narrowest penthouse, the lowest openings, the most finely-angled tambour and the slowest walls.

Les and I decided to try for the job in Melbourne. I applied, at the same time, for the position that had fallen vacant at Hampton Court, but the Australians were so much more enthusiastic in their response that I withdrew from the latter application. For some reason there were no other approaches to the Royal Melbourne Tennis Club and, after much letter-writing, the appointment was made.

Six months of notice were required at Oxford, but this was no real problem as the Melbourne Club was still building the new complex. Mick Dean was appointed as my successor. I sought advice from my old mentor, Peter Dawes, who was of the opinion that Australia was a good idea as long as I practised hard by myself and only stayed there for two years.

Just before leaving I managed to reach the quarter-final of the British Open Singles (then called the Field Trophy) by pipping David Johnson 6-4 in the fifth set, before being crushed by Norwood Cripps, who went on to win the tournament.

CHAPTER 20

MELBOURNE

We packed our bags, leapt on a 'plane and landed at Melbourne at 6 a.m. on the 5th December, 1973. Even at that unearthly hour the Club President, Richard Allen and his right-hand man, George Limb, were there to meet us. At 8.30 a.m. I was attending the weekly site meeting in Richmond, where progress on the new construction was being reviewed. Progress was actually very poor. The decision to rebuild had been taken in 1971 and work should have been completed early in 1973, but there had been frustrating delays before planning permission was given, and this meant that the building programme ran on into a particularly bad, strike-affected period in Australian history. Colin Gurney and Eric Godfrey were the Committee men with the onerous task of overseeing the work and keeping the pressure on the builders. Even so, it was obvious that I would be working for some considerable time at the old Melbourne court.

The Melbourne Tennis Club had been built in 1882 at 345 Exhibition Street, which is on a corner of the city's centre block. It wasn't the first court to be built in Australia: one had been and gone in Ballaarat, and the Hobart court had been constructed seven years earlier. The Melbourne Tennis Club had had its ups and downs, receiving a royal charter and nearly closing four times. In 1973 it was a solid Victorian building containing the tennis court, two squash courts and an indoor swimming pool.

The decision to move was a remarkably brave and shrewd one taken by Richard Allen, and endorsed by his Committee. The old building was starting to run up huge bills and was struggling, as it had struggled for many years, to keep its financial head above water. The deal struck by Richard Allen not only wiped out the Club's considerable overdraft and gave it brand new premises three times the size of the original; it also enabled the Club to have continuous tennis because, although paying in advance, the purchaser of the Exhibition Street site had to wait until completion of the new complex before taking possession.

That was the shrewd part. The brave part was to undertake the construction of a tennis club for the first time anywhere in the world for over fifty years, in a rather poor suburb of a city that had barely supported a court in an ideal location, and to build not just one, but two tennis courts. Was this sensible? Were they constructing a folly - a monument to some outdated game? Would the balls bounce properly on a modern surface? Richard Allen adopted what he called the turtle

107

principle: the only way to advance is to stick your neck out. The tennis world is grateful to him, not only because he gave us a new tennis facility, but also because he gave us a model. Other courts have been built in the last century near the centres of towns that have since grown into cities, on sites which have become valuable real estate, just like Melbourne. Already Bordeaux has followed this example, by moving from their city property to a nearby suburb, and the game is secure in Aquitane for a while, as a result.

Les and I worked hard at the Exhibition Street court. There hadn't been a professional there since Woolner Stone died, a decade earlier; only a series of club managers. Woolner had been an institution, serving the Club for sixty-three years man and boy, and his father Thomas had also given half a life-time. Bearing in mind that we were about to transfer to larger facilities, our job was to expand membership and promote tennis until the big move. Court usage was running at thirty-two hours a week when we arrived and we quickly built this up to around sixty hours per week. After ten years without a pro there were many members keen to have lessons.

The delays and frustrations went on and on and it was another nine months before we finally moved to Richmond. Not that we were bored: there was plenty to do, a new country to see - and Les was pregnant.

Early in 1974 there ambled into my life one of the men who have had the most influence on it. The amble was the fastest gait possible for Barry Toates, the others being a shuffle, a dawdle and a stop. Bazza, as he is affectionately known, had been born in the same Mill Road Hospital in Cambridge as myself, but nine months earlier. Assistant professional at Cambridge for two and a half years, he had then boarded an Italian boat bound for Australia when still shy of his eighteenth birthday, in order to become the professional at Hobart. Everybody loved him and over six or seven years he had raised court usage to a miraculous eighty hours a week in peak season.

In those days Barry never did anything in a hurry. Bookings started at 7 a.m., so he used to get there at six to clean the court. Using a fifteen-inch broom instead of the more sensible four-foot variety and moving like a lethargic chameleon he used to take a full hour to do a five-minute job.

Mind you, he could play beautiful tennis and he certainly taught me a lot. At that stage I knew about the cutting game and the forcing game, but I had never seen the length game used to such deadly effect. Our first encounter was in the final of the Australian Open of 1974 and although I managed to sneak the third set when two sets behind, Barry crushed me 6-0 in the fourth. His principle is to make his opponents play the ball after it has struck first the floor and then a side wall, whenever possible. Although this tactic will gain few outright winners, it will force a great number of errors, present his opponent with a ball that is difficult to attack, and consequently slow down the pace of the game. You may ask why we don't all adopt this tactic. The answer is that we don't all have Barry's control and temperament. Playing the ball accurately to a length is often easy enough when returning serve, but when under pressure and at full stretch by the grille it is a different kettle of fish. Few of us are calm enough in this sort of situation to produce such control.

Barry achieves this not only because he is the unflappable type but as a result of sound technique. He times the movements of his feet into the corners to perfection, doesn't panic or snatch at the ball, and keeps his wrist disciplined. He slides the ball over the net with only enough backspin to aid his control and to keep the ball low; very rarely does he force or cut heavily, although he is well capable of doing so on occasion.

I was so impressed with Barry's length game that, for a while, I more or less discarded everything else to concentrate on it. My results in that period were mediocre at best, as I painfully discovered that gliding into corners and caressing the ball would not make a silk purse out of this particular pig's ear. For all that, the studied concentration on control made me a better player overall, and I would thoroughly recommend it to anyone with the time and ambition to become a competent, all-round player.

The first time I saw Barry practise he was rolling balls off the penthouse above the dedans and, after the bounce, he was chipping them over the net as short as he could. To my amazement and seemingly contrary to the laws of parabolic flight, he was capable of dropping the ball on to hazard chase the door, and at medium pace too. By the time the ball reached the back wall it was rolling. This is an excellent training routine, with an element of fun in it as you try to clip your shot ever closer to the net without erring. The same thing can be done with the patting exercise - pat the ball down into the back wall and then slip it over the net as short as you can.

The advantages Barry gains with his control are many. The mistakes induced by his nagging length start to undermine his adversary's confidence after a while and, because he seldom gives you a downright easy ball to kill, a feeling of impotence will creep in. His opponents become aware of their inferior control and may resort to desperation

Barry Toates

tactics, such as all-out forcing. If you do succumb to this, Barry will never fail to give you a disarming grin after each force, just to let you know how worried he is. Above all you will find that, if you are not careful, you are playing him at his own game and at his pace and tempo. If this happens you might as well pack your bags and go home, because Barry's tempo is in keeping with the rest of his functions. He wanders languidly around the court during play and changes ends like a somnambulist.

There was a time when he tried to take his length game a stage further. Instead of hitting the floor at last gallery and the side wall at chase three and four, he would pitch the ball on to the second gallery line so that it was dying on the side wall around chase four and five. This meant that not only was his opponent scraping the ball off the side wall as usual, he was also stretching forwards and hitting upwards, making his return even more ineffective. This tactic never really paid off for Barry though because, having induced his opponent into a weak reply, instead of putting the ball away Barry would play a similar teaser to the other side.

This, then, is the major pitfall to avoid when striving to improve your length game: do not start pushing. Most good players have been through a stage of pushing the ball to a good length, instead of stroking it there, and allowing themselves to become completely negative, in the hope that their opponents will make enough mistakes to lose on the percentages. Singles at tennis is an attacking game and whether you are playing heavy cut, forcing for openings or stroking for length, you should do it with the positive intention of winning the point, rather than trying to avoid losing it. If you are playing defensively then too often you will find that you are 'unlucky' and your opponent hits the corner of the tambour, finds a nick or floats one into the grille.

How do you combat a player such as Barry Toates? Unless you can match him for control the only solution is to disrupt his rhythm in some way. Force a little more than usual, put a bit more weight into your cut strokes, aim for the galleries more often in order to keep the rests short and the changes of ends more frequent. Apply pressure as best you can, but in moderation. The two disastrous courses are desperation slogging and allowing yourself to be drawn into his game. This advice is relevant at any level of the game where two comparable players are battling for psychological supremacy.

1974 wound its course and brought us a son, Ivan, in August. In September we finally moved into the new Royal Melbourne Tennis Club in Sherwood Street, Richmond. It was a turbulent time and, being a cantankerous sort, I had had my differences of opinion with the

Club Committee. However there were some great men among them and I learned a lot from them. The night before the new club actually opened, Richard Allen and I spent four hours dismantling the packages of furniture that had been sent to us in kit form, screwing the pieces together and installing them in the club rooms. There was tension between us then and we worked in stony silence, save for one isolated comment half-way through the evening. 'You know,' said Richard, not looking up from the coffee table he was bent over, 'It's a terrible thing to be right all the time. Makes you very unpopular'.

I had trained diligently throughout that year, so when I returned to Britain in November in order to play in the British Open (which had changed its name from the previous year to the Cutty Sark Invitation tournament) a big improvement was expected. I lost in the quarter-final to Howard Angus by 3-2. By this I mean that he won three sets and I garnered two games. The real score was 6-1, 6-0, 6-1, and the manner of his victory was devastating. I couldn't see how I could ever achieve that standard and all my training appeared to have had no effect on my ranking in Britain. Perhaps I had made a mistake in leaving the Northern Hemisphere, where most of the competition was. I returned to Australia with my tail between my legs and, although the training continued, I had almost abandoned any thoughts of making it to the top.

Over Easter in 1975 there was a tennis festival in Australia - the official opening of the new Royal Melbourne Tennis Club by Lord Aberdare and the celebration of the centenary of the Hobart Tennis Club. It was then that I discovered that progress in tennis is rarely made along a smooth, rising path but rather in a series of plateaux. Suddenly the gap between the world's leading exponents and myself had been cut in half. The message, dear reader, is not to be disheartened if your attempts to improve appear to fail. Provided the practice is constructive those quantum leaps will come, but in their own good time. Much the same can be said about receiving tuition. Unless the strokes you are learning are services or volleys, do not expect an immediate transformation. Take your lessons philosophically, concentrate on what you have been taught and eventually the goods will be delivered.

Back-tracking a few months: Colin Lumley became my first Australian assistant late in 1974, a few days before his seventeenth birthday. Left-handed, tenacious and fiery, he became fanatical about practising and was quickly carving his way through the ranks of the Melbourne amateurs. He also picked up the fundamental tasks of being a

Colin Lumley

professional in no time at all. Awl blades and needles flew everywhere as rackets and balls rolled hot off the production line.

There was no doubt about it: the new Club was a roaring success. There were teething problems of course, but nothing serious and new members were flocking to play this game that had almost died in Australia ten or fifteen years earlier. Women started playing in the mornings, businessmen filled the lunch-time and early evening hours and, because the Club was modern and plush, the younger set were attracted there in the evenings. It is a real problem in tennis that so few clubs have the social facilities that attract young blood, and hence that so few play the game in their most athletic years.

Over the New Year period Barry Toates and I played a twenty-four hour fund-raising marathon for the Easter jamboree. We were sponsored for each set played, each grille hit etc. and we raised some $890. We also had a side bet on the result, so the match was played competitively for the whole time. By the end Barry had blisters three deep on each foot and my right forearm had had to be put in a temporary plaster. I won the bet by twenty-two sets to nineteen but, more importantly, I received a twenty-four hour lesson from a great artist, the impressions of which have never left me.

This was a magical time for Australian tennis. It could boast the fullest courts in the world and the best rate of improvement of the general amateur standard. There was talk of courts all round Australasia and a sense of momentum in the air. The Melbourne opening and the Hobart centenary were wonderful advertisements for the Australian impetus of the time and most were genuinely impressed. Every day held a feast of tennis with the Bathurst Cup, the Governor's Cup and a host of level, handicap, singles, doubles, graded and open events being staged. Every night there was a social do somewhere and one had to be fit to stay with the pace.

My fortunes as a player took a turn for the better that fortnight, for a couple of big scalps came my way. In the Melbourne opening tournament I defeated both Northrup Knox and Norwood Cripps before losing in the final to Frank Willis by 6-4 in the fifth set. Northrup Knox - there was a name to conjure with. Norty had been an outstanding World Champion, reigning for ten years and then retiring undefeated. David Cull, the Lords professional, tells how Norty travelled to Britain to help his compatriot, Pete Bostwick, win the vacant world title against Frank Willis, the British challenger, in 1969. The two Americans were playing practice sets at Lords and, according to David, Norty was just fooling around and still winning. It appeared that he could do anything he wanted with the ball. Even allowing for the fact that, unlike Pete, he had no mental pressures, and even if the account were only half true, this was an incredible performance against the man who was about to assume the title and hold it with distinction.

It was hard to spot distinctive aspects of Norty's technique but he was certainly a very aggressive player. It was the first time I had seen anyone deliberately playing for the back wall nick, especially on the volley. From thirty yards range it might seem rather ambitious to aim for a target only a few inches in height, but bearing in mind the difficulty of the alternatives - volleying to a length or for an opening and the risks involved in doing so - the nick-volley becomes more feasible. Of course it helps if you can find your target as often as Norty did.

From the point of view of the tournament it was unfortunate that six years had elapsed during which Norty had played very little, and I was able to scrape through. That result, plus defeating Norwood Cripps in the semi-final and extending Frank Willis to five sets in the final, was heady stuff for me, but the euphoria evaporated the following week when I lost to Alan Lovell at Hobart. That was when the value of home court advantage was brought home to me and the realisation came through that, although I had beaten the likes of Norwood Cripps, it was on my court, with my balls, in front of my own crowd. On a neutral court I would have lost. Alan Lovell was more my mark, but even that was not a bad mark and represented improvement.

A common problem with tennis players is the fact that it is difficult to be physically relaxed and yet remain mentally alert. With balls popping at you from short range off the back wall and the tambour, it is important to have relaxed muscles that allow your elbow and knees to flex at the last moment. Yet become too relaxed and you find yourself getting casual and sloppy. On the other hand if you concentrate like mad, often your muscles will seize up and you end up looking like a clumsy puppet. The answer is to find the middle road - and that means practice.

A similar paradox exists with beginners and players of moderate experience who try to stop themselves from snatching at balls in the corners. The remedy is to start your stroke a fraction earlier and then to swing more slowly. Unfortunately, while concentrating on swinging slowly, most competitors find that they start running slowly as well, so that they don't even reach the ball in the corner. More practice!

The icing on the cake that Easter was the presence of that remarkable man Pierre Etchebaster. Much has already been written about Pierre and his retirement, aged almost sixty, undefeated, from twenty-six years as world champion. It was said that even then, in 1975, at the age of eighty-one, he was difficult to beat in a solitary set. He commanded sufficient respect for Norty Knox and himself to be top seeds in the doubles event, ahead of Frank Willis and Norwood Cripps. He never played, sadly, for he had swollen ankles, but for two weeks he delighted us with his courteous advice and amusing recollections. He also gave a couple of clinics, each attended by some eighty enthusiasts, and allowed us an insight into his undoubted mastery. The ease and fluency with which he demonstrated the volley from the penthouse, in particular, were extraordinary. The balls flew from a racket that appeared to have struck them soundlessly.

The holiday was over and we all went back to work. Richard Allen resigned as President of the R.M.T.C. and his place was taken by George Limb. Here was a real gentleman and a master of diplomacy in tight situations. A fine amateur player, George plays in a free-hitting fashion and always performs better in a match than in a friendly. This is not only because of his excellent match temperament but also because in matches there are markers, whereas in friendlies he calls the chases himself and invariably errs in favour of his adversary. In addition, he used to announce a double hit whenever the ball came off the wood of his racket, which wasn't often anyway.

My favourite story about George concerns the occasion when I had just posted the draws for the graded club championship on the notice-board. As the second-ranked player in the Club George would normally have expected his name to be one of the sixteen in the 'A' Grade draw. However the tournaments sub-committee had agreed a rule which exempted the holders of the Club's Gold Racket and Silver Racket prizes from playing in 'A' Grade. The winner of that competition would challenge them for their titles at the end of the season. George did not know this. He came into the club, saw the competition sheets on the board and went to look for his name and draw. On discovering that he was not in 'A' Grade he proceeded to look down the thirty-two names in 'B' Grade, and he had started on the 'C' Grade list before I came over and advised him of the new ruling. He did admit to me that he had decided that he was going to be annoyed if he was in 'C' Grade.

It was a measure of the rapid expansion of the Club that, only four months after Colin Lumley became an assistant, my request for a second junior professional was granted immediately. Lachlan Deuchar was selected from the six hopefuls who applied for the position. I often wonder how some of the others would have fared.

Lachie, as he is known, was then sixteen and a half years old, less than a year younger than Colin. Both were young, Australian, sports-loving males, but within that framework they were as different as chalk and cheese. Colin would bustle into the club each morning, go straight to the court and cut balls until his arm went limp, and then spend the next six or seven hours furiously attacking the balls and rackets that needed attention in the pro shop. He worked hard and expected others to do so too. His temper was brittle and he needed pretty delicate handling.

By contrast, Lachie would meander lackadaisically into the club at a compromise time between when he was expected and what suited him, had to be bullied into training and was quite content to lounge about the club rooms all day, doing nothing but chat to the members. He needed to be kicked into action all the time and showed no traces of responsibility, but with his easy-going disposition he was almost impossible to offend.

In some ways they were a good combination from the point of view of management. While Colin bore the brunt of the work-load required of them, Lachie's role as public relations officer in the bar was not without its merit. And if ever an emergency arose, such as a flood in the changing-room, it was always Lachie who had nothing better to do that evening and cheerfully offered to lend a hand for two or three hours.

Despite this, something had to be done about Lachie's indolence, and at the start of each working week forty old balls were placed in his drawer for recovering by the week's end. Lachie worked Sunday to Thursday inclusive but Sundays and balls did not seem to go together for him. In a typical week he might do one on Monday, another on Tuesday, an animated three balls on the Wednesday, and then cancel his plans for Thursday evening and sit up until 5 a.m. completing his quota.

Colin, who religiously pumped out eight balls a day no matter what, was aghast at Lachie's attitude to life and work. The feeling was mutual. They didn't get on, those two, and would undoubtedly have come to blows but for Lachie's infinite capacity for absorbing the kaleidoscopic assortment of insults that Colin flung at him, with just a shrug of the shoulders. For a bloke unrenowned for his linguistic talents in normal life, Colin had an alarmingly colourful vocabulary when it came to abuse.

Both have now matured into fine young men and both made, and are still making, very real contributions to the game. They even like each other now. Well, sort of. In that sense it was worth all the hassles and headaches of guiding them through their respective apprenticeships.

In general, though, I am opposed to the practice of selecting sixteen- and seventeen-year olds for induction into the ranks of tennis professionals. This used to be common policy in Britain for centuries and that doyen of British tennis, Henry Johns, tells how, when he was a lad, if ever a vacancy occurred on the professional staff of a London tennis club, there would be a queue of boys clamouring to demonstrate their proficiency and dexterity with the tools of the trade.

117

More recently, there has been a dearth of competition amongst eager striplings wishing to take up apprenticeships. Too often those who are found are unsuitable, untalented or too immature to see life ahead clearly. The fact is that a modern professional is required not only to mark, coach, sew balls and string rackets as of yore but also to manage the day-to-day running of the club. Any such competent person who is a professional knows full well that were he to turn his attentions to another racket sport, such as squash, and devote the same amount of energy to it, then he would reap far greater financial rewards. So why does he stick to tennis? Either because of a deep-rooted passion for the game, or because of ambition as a competitor, or both.

Take a twenty-year-old, preferably one who has played tennis as an amateur, and you have an individual whose competence and potential can be assessed in a few weeks, whose training can be as short as a few months, and who goes into the job with his eyes open and with no illusions about what the future holds.

On the other hand, the average youth who is three or four years younger than that has only the vaguest notion about the direction his life will take, needs about three years of development, and may turn out to be completely the wrong sort of chap anyway. And there you are, with a half-trained professional who will contribute little to tennis while he, poor bloke, nurses the idea that perhaps he could have been a brilliant neuro-surgeon if he hadn't wasted his time footling about with something that wasn't his bag, if only he'd been mature enough to realise it. Another minus when training teenagers is that you have to go through the final stages of adolescence with them: just spots, girls and moodiness if you are lucky; drink, drugs and pilfering if you are not.

So I salute you, Colin Lumley and Lachie Deuchar; but I wouldn't want to go through it all again.

Another year rolled away, bringing a second son, Ben, born in March 1976. By the end of that year Barry Toates was six-one up on me in matches and I set myself to try to defeat him in the final of the Tasmanian Open. A low spot loomed ahead, unbeknown to me. I did not even reach the final, losing the semi- to Graham Hyland by 0-6, 6-4, 6-3. We had entered five tournaments together before then. Graham had always thrashed me in practice before them, but I had won each of the five semi-finals by a large margin in scoring terms. Graham, however, had tremendous talent and I had felt that if he had just managed to find a toe-hold in any of those matches, we would have been in for a dog-fight. In this sixth semi-final I led 6-0 and 4-2 when he got his foot in the door, and then he was away and not to be caught that day.

Let me tell you about this fellow Graham Hyland. Someone once observed to me that to be a successful tennis pro you had to be either a great player or a great character. Well, Graham is a great player and he is also an out-and-out, raving, head-banging ding-bat.

He started his career as assistant to Barry Toates in Hobart in March 1973. Before that he used to go to school, but only when the fancy took him. He had been a successful student until home-work started up. That, apparently, was out of the question. He used to catch the bus to school each day and, with a hundred yards to go, would decide then what sort of day lay ahead. Half the time he stayed on the bus and went on to the local library, where he spent the day reading about one of his two passions, Red Indians and cricket. The other half he would go to school and proceed straight to the gymnasium and games area, and join in whatever sport was available that day - but preferably cricket. Just occasionally he would make up his mind to attend a class and would do his level best to understand what was going on. If something was beyond him he would ask for an explanation and, if that wasn't clear enough, he would press for more, but at the first sign of intolerance or criticism from the teacher he would get up and walk out. It is difficult to comprehend how eccentric Graham was unless you had met him.

He is a fine sportsman. At badminton he rose to the top of the Australian tree, impeded only by his brushes with officialdom. As a batsman he had the potential to play for his country had he stuck at it. There is something inside Graham, however, that makes him shy away from the pinnacles of sport, just when he seems about to achieve them. He gave up both badminton and cricket just before they could have made him famous. A few years later he was to quit serious tennis a couple of months after winning the U.S. Open and when the top honours beckoned him.

Tremendously quick over short distances, Graham is sinewy and athletic. One of the contests we used to hold on party nights was the penthouse run. This consisted of standing on the penthouse above the grille and running full tilt along all three penthouses, finishing at the main wall above the dedans. The best time for this event was seven and a half seconds - impressive when you remember that the distance is over sixty yards, run on a course angled at, perhaps, twenty-five degrees. It was dangerous, too, especially if alcohol was being consumed, and arms and wrists have been broken from crashes in Australia. Graham once ran the course in reverse after a dinner at the R.M.T.C., starting above the dedans to give the spectators a view of the finish. Going like a bolt of lightning he was half-way in no time, but when he tried to cut a corner by leaping across the angle between the service penthouse and the grille penthouse, he lost his footing and tripped. Instead of sprawling and crashing to the floor, he somersaulted on to the grille penthouse, rolled sideways twice, and vaulted to the ground. He was disqualified from the run, but received high marks for artistic interpretation.

For all his athletic prowess, Graham's eyes were poor. Without prior knowledge he could not recognise a stationary opponent at the other end of a court. In the light of this, being driven in a car by him was an even more frightening experience. He used to commute to work in Hobart some seventeen miles of very long, steep hills, in his old mini-van. The speedometer on the vehicle only went up to ninety miles per hour, but on the down slopes Graham would have the needle way past that and half-way through the petrol gauge. Worse, by far, was his habit of reading comics on the steering wheel as he was driving, leaving only his peripheral vision for the road.

Graham had an obsession with the American Indians, their life-style and their codes of honour. This was no passing craze but a real religion to him. He read whatever material was available on the subject and even adopted the Indian name of the man he revered most - Tashunka Witko, I think it was - Crazy Horse to the rest of us.

The wide open spaces, the horses, the freedom and the proud dignity of these fine people all appealed to Graham, and he resented the manner in which they had been subjugated by chicanery and gun-fire. In fact, there was a period when he refused to talk to a white man for three months, which was no trifling matter when you were employed in a white man's club. If the 'phone rang and no one else was available to answer he would just pick up the receiver and listen. If the caller said nothing he would hang up, and if there were a message he would write it down for Barry. This was not the only peculiar form of answering the 'phone that he had, simply the worst. Apart from that silent stage there were others when he would answer with 'Speak' or, after a few moments of pause while the caller waited for a response: 'Well, go on then - you're paying for it.'

We used to call Graham 'Half-measures Hyland' as a cynical reference to his habit of talking in absolutes: 'That was the worst shot anyone has ever played at any sport.'; 'You are the ugliest person who has ever lived,' (usually directed at me); or 'I'll never speak to him again - ever,' said of someone who had just slighted him in some insignificant or imagined way.

120

Graham's relationship with Barry was an interesting one. They had great respect for one another, but even Bazza was a white man to Graham and underwent the treatment. They were complete opposites in many ways. One was slow, methodical and even-tempered while the other was all speed, spontaneity and hostility.

Many years later Graham described to me the start of his intransigent stage. He and Barry had booked a court for practice one day and, when the hour had come, Graham had left the pro shop for the court with Barry's assurance that he would be there in a minute. But, as usual, it took Barry twenty minutes to get himself into gear, while his assistant impatiently bashed balls around the court. At the moment he did arrive, Graham was doubled over and rubbing his eyes, for some reason. Barry took his position at the service end and prepared to knock a ball over the net, when Graham suddenly uncoiled and started blinking at the court around him, his eyes sore from the intense massage and unaccustomed to the light. 'You ready?' asked Barry, and that was it. Graham marched off the court without saying a word and wouldn't speak to anyone for three months.

I asked him to describe to me a typical day. 'Well,' he replied, 'I had to be in at nine. Committee said so. But I didn't go with that so the first hour I just sat and read comics. Barry'd been there since six or seven or some bloody hour. He'd be sitting by the 'phone, one elbow on the table, chin resting in hand, staring at the booking sheet. Ten o'clock come and I'd go out and get some doughnuts. Read some more till eleven. Look up. Barry'd still be looking at the booking sheet. Get the balls out and tie like a bastard till me fingers went numb. Bazza still staring. Maybe he's got himself a cup of tea by now. Chap comes in for a lesson. Barry tells him to go on court and he'll follow in a minute. Then stares at booking sheet for another twenty minutes without moving a muscle. Eventually sighs, gets up, finishes his tea, finds a racket, gives booking sheet one last wistful look and wanders off to give a lesson......'

Graham was one of those guys who could get away with murder. Some members adored him and would do anything for him. Others detested him and swore they'd get him for his latest dastardly act, but somehow they always ended up by forgiving him and trying to win him over. There was something very Tasmanian about him, and the Hobart members were not going to kick him out for simply insulting all the Committee members or refusing to speak for three months.

Graham has a great gift for impersonations in terms of action. These would range from an imitation of the Club President at a social gathering to a demonstration of the Club's worst player attempting his first railroad. His best impressions, though, were of famous cricketers, such as Slasher McKay, Ian Redpath - and any English batsman being struck on the body by Jeff Thomson. I was particularly impressed by his Gary Sobers bowling the quicker stuff, left-handed and all.

Undoubtedly this improved his popularity and was also of great value when coaching tennis. Graham only had to watch players for a few minutes before being able to mimic them. This meant that he could show a pupil exactly how Pierre Etchebaster would play a forehand to the grille and, even more usefully, he could act as a three-dimensional re-play video and demonstrate just how his pupil had played the same stroke, faults included. He had a real flair for coaching, a combination of knowledge, analysis and exuberance. If the student was someone he related to well, the hour would zip by, with Graham talking nineteen to the dozen and his pupil drinking in every word, confident that by next week he would be in 'A' Grade.

Graham is a lovely player to watch. His footwork can be exemplary and there is always a sense of poise and balance about him. In his early years he would get down so low, and keep the head of the racket so high above his wrist, that the cut he put on the ball produced more sidespin than underspin and the ball would swerve yards in the air. This almost became a handicap to him because he was committed to going cross-court on return of service.

He is one of the few serious players who appreciate the art and artistry of serving. A lot of the big boys have a railroad, a sidewall, an underarm twist, a high service and a bobble, but that's it. There is no subtlety in their serving, whereas Graham understands that, for example, throwing the ball a fraction further left on the underarm results in the application of just a touch of topspin, which his opponent might mis-read by only six inches, hook the ball very slightly on to the main wall in compensation and lose the point two or three strokes later, without ever realising that it was the masked spin which got him off to a poor start in the rest.

It is very easy to develop an inferiority complex when competing against Graham. He darts about, exuding confidence, probing for openings. Great tracts of time can elapse before he makes a mistake. However there are chinks, even in *his* armour. One is his tendency to play wristy shots, especially if he is under pressure. Some put this down to his badminton training, and that may be true, but it is something that afflicts him only in passages.

Graham Hyland

Another is his susceptibility to innovation. I once mused with him, just before a tournament, what a racket would feel like if the three inches below the grip were removed, leaving a shorter instrument which would be held at the end, as one does at any other racket game. Graham immediately volunteered to try it, found a saw and lopped a few inches off the handle of one his rackets. He then went on court, played a set with it and pronounced it a winner. So what does Half-measures Hyland do? He only totally commits himself by performing similar surgery on his other three rackets. Unfortunately for him, as the tournament approached his wonderful play gradually deteriorated because, while the implement felt light and manoeuvrable, it also accentuated his inclination for wristy flicks. He lost.

Just before the 1975 Easter functions, rumours were emanating from Hobart that Graham was beating Barry in practice 6-0, 6-1 - and regularly. In the first round of the Melbourne tournament he was drawn to play Alan Lovell and those of us resident in Australia fancied him to register a shock win. What we didn't reckon with was Graham bumping into Pierre Etchebaster for the first time on the day before the match. Pierre gave Graham a verbal lesson on how he used to play the ball with an open stance, dropped racket head and no cut - almost diametrically opposite to what Barry had been telling him for two years. Graham decided to try this new theory out, not in practice, oh no! - but in his match with Alan. Despite looking every inch how we imagined a rusty Pierre must have looked, he lost another match that he really should have won.

His improvisation knew no bounds. He once devised a method of returning railroads by standing on the ledge of hazard second gallery, hooking his right arm round the hazard second post, and swinging at the ball with a left-handed backhand while it was still on the penthouse. It sounds farcical and it was certainly amusing but, because of his agility, it was very difficult to adjust the service so as to put it out of his reach, or suddenly to deliver a different service without his leaping from the ledge back to a more conventional position.

A different flaw in Graham's make-up was his physical conditioning. This was deceptive, because one could hardly wish for a more agile, speedy and fit player: his badminton training saw to that. No, his problem was that after a couple of hours of hard play, if his opponent survived that long, his stamina would be found wanting. His legs would feel tired and the tell-tale sign for this was his bending of his knees individually, by lifting his heel towards his backside, between points. The effect would not be dramatic but the sparkle would fade from his game and, being tired, he appeared to run out of fresh ideas, so that by the end he was often just going through the motions. This in turn meant that he lost some confidence in himself as a good match player, because his lack of stamina resulted in him losing a few matches from winning positions. Both problems diminished over the years because, as with most athletes, maturity brought a slight lessening in speed, but greater staying power.

As I was saying, Graham beat me in the semi-final of the Tasmanian Open of 1976 and almost beat his mentor, Barry, in the final, losing 2-6, 6-5, 6-5, after leading 6-2, 4-2, 40-15, serving and with a ball on the dedans penthouse. After only three and a half years of play he had done himself proud. A few weeks later, right out of the blue, he resigned his job at the Hobart Tennis Club.

I had decided to make my first trip to America instead of going to Britain that season. Almost all my holidays were taken up with going to overseas tournaments, which wasn't very fair on the wife, except when she came along too. Starting from Britain, I have made eight trips to Australia to date, plus eleven to the United States and any number to France. Contrary to popular notion, the vast majority of these voyages have been self-financed and despite some success over the years, I have made an enormous net loss. This was always going to be the case, so there is no remorse about it. I am only one of many professionals who love playing international tournaments and who do so knowing full well that these competitions cost money, not just in expenses, but also in lost coaching fees back home. Until recently only the world championship itself was a real money-spinner and even then only if it was held in your own country. Fortunately for us a lucrative pro-am event has been inaugurated in America by Peter de Svastich; and the difference made by the sponsorship of the British game by Unigate, and subsequently by George Wimpey, has been dramatic. Not only are the major events well padded but the smaller handicap events, which are so important to the younger pros, are supported and sustained. In addition, the staging costs for amateur events are being covered by Wimpey and never has there been such a full and healthy tennis calendar in Britain.

I wanted this first trip to the States to be a successful one and, as Graham had made himself redundant, he agreed to come over to Melbourne and assist with my preparation, in return for a bed and a daily supply of steaks, oranges and chocolate bars. It was good to have someone with such a range of knowledge as a training partner, and beneficial that he would insist on another ten court sprints when my legs were telling me that enough was enough.

After six weeks of this I packed my suitcase and left for New York. Leaving behind temperatures of over ninety degrees, I was greeted by nights of minus fifteen degrees and days that were barely less harsh. Tennis in America was a much more exclusive game than elsewhere in the world, I was to discover, and few indeed were permitted access to its charms.

Norwood Cripps

The U.S. Professional Singles was held in New York and Norwood Cripps saw me off in the final. Norwood was a mercurial sort of player.

126

I doubt if he lost a friendly match at any time during the 'seventies, because in these games he seemed unplayable. When practising with him I used to receive fifteen and still didn't ever win sets. My best cross-court returns of serve would be swept disdainfully into the winning gallery. But somehow it was often different in a match, and if Norwood was under pressure the wheels used to come off. He was one of the greatest doubles players though and it was easy to see why. His three relative weaknesses at singles were his slowness around the court, his suspect backhand and his pessimism if the going got tough. With a partner like Alan Lovell taking the left side of the court there was no need for him to be speedy, he hardly ever played backhands and he could be fortified by his partner in the tight spots. In fact, he and Alan were undefeated for the first seven years of their union, winning nine straight major doubles titles.

The next event was the U.S. Open Singles, held at the Philadelphia Racquet Club. The athletic department of this city club was dominated by a dinosaur called Jimmy Dunn. Jimmy was a professional there for some fifty-five years and was a rough, tough, colourful type. He told his members what he thought of them to their faces and there weren't many who felt indifferent about him. Like Henry Johns, he was at his best when yarning about the old days and the old stars, and I spent many happy hours listening to his tales. Pierre Etchebaster was someone he respected but didn't get along with, and his idol was the great Jock Soutar, a stocky little rackets player with arms that hung down to his knees. Jimmy had been a fair player himself, with the best doubles record in the country. 'You .... modern players cut the .... ball too .... much,' he snapped at me. 'Cut comes fourth. That's what Pierre used to say. First height, second length, third direction and fourth cut.' By all accounts both he and Pierre used to hit like stink in their hey-days.

Jimmy told me that he had had twenty-five assistants in the previous thirty years. Only two were left in the game and, indeed, many careers of American professionals seem to be short. Perhaps it is the life-style in their big city clubs, or the lack of competitive play - or maybe it is simply insufficient financial reward.

The Philadelphia court is a beautiful one to look at and has the best lighting anywhere. From the playing point of view its most distinctive feature is the abrasive floor, which is very tiring on the legs and produces long, slow rests - the clay court of tennis, as Ralph Howe would drawl. The rough floor also dissipates spin and this reduces the incentive to attack with cut, for the ball will seldom come down sharply off the back wall.

In the bottom half of the draw I took my revenge against Norwood Cripps, who had beaten me the previous week in the U.S. Professional Championships. I led by two sets to love and 4-1 in games; but Norwood came back strongly and I didn't win until the fifth set. The seeds in the top half were Gene Scott and Ralph Howe, the two men who have dominated U.S. amateur tennis for the last decade. Off court Ralph is a charming gentleman and most amusing with his dry humour and telling observations. A master of the understatement, one gathers his point of view not only from his comments but also from his fractionally-raised eyebrows, the minutest angling of his jaw, the studied adjustment of his glasses with the left fore-finger. On court he is remarkable because of his firm hitting, very clean and flat - and because he is the only man who can keep Barry Toates waiting.

In the quarter-final Ralph was drawn to meet Jimmy Burke, the up-and-coming nineteen-year old Philadelphia assistant pro. They were quite a contrast: Jimmy bustling about the court with ants in his pants, while Ralph casually sauntered around, taking his time. Ralph had been half an hour late for the match anyway, having played in a squash tournament earlier in the day, and in the middle of the second set he suddenly disappeared to change his green-and-white hooped shirt for a pink one. As this took a full twenty minutes the spectators became incensed, got behind Jimmy and cheered him to victory.

This took Jimmy into a semi-final against the top seed, Gene Scott, who had won the title for the previous five years. Gene beat him in four sets and then defeated me by the same margin in the final. Gene was probably the best tournament player in the world at that time for, although Howard Angus had twice defeated him in World Championship matches, in each case Gene had been the first to reach three sets (3-1 in the first case, 3-0 in the second).

Part of his prowess was the shock factor, because he was the only player of the day who volleyed so much and who hit the ball so hard. He was, and is, disconcerting to play because it is difficult to tell whether or not he is trying. It is almost as if he needs the motivation of being 2-4 down in the final set before his engine fires on all cylinders. Even then there is little change in his outward expression or movement, but you can tell by the way the dedans net starts to billow.

Back in Australia, Barry Toates decided to give the rest of us a chance by getting married. The effects were so immediate that in the

Gene Scott

Tasmanian Open Graham Hyland beat Barry for the first time ever in a match, although it took three hard sets to do so. This was a real milestone for Graham and he celebrated so vigorously that night that he could hardly stand up the next day, and I had no trouble winning the final.

Shortly afterwards I recorded my first triumph in a major event by toppling Barry in the Australian Open Singles. It was the end of an era for Barry. He had won that championship nine times in a row before this loss, he had wedded, and he was shortly to leave Australia for his new appointment in Boston after ten and a half years in Hobart. Karen, his bride, had wrought a few changes in him. He had learned how to lie in of a morning, how to walk moderately fast in order to keep up with her, and that he had better not muck about too much in a match in case she stormed out of the dedans in high dudgeon, which was not unknown.

Barry was capable of lovely touches of humour, even at critical points during a match. He was once playing rather poorly against Chris Ennis in the British Open of 1975 and kept winking to the full dedans, as if he had the situation under control and was just about to launch an offensive. When he finally became match point down, the members of

129

the press got up rather noisily in search of the bar. Barry was changing ends to defend a chase at the time and saw them leaving. 'Oi,' he shouted at the disappearing backs. 'You're going to miss the exciting bit!' He was renowned for his escapes from the brink of defeat, but although he extended the match for a few minutes, he did lose that day.

On another occasion he was playing Colin Lumley in a handicap match and, after a bad start, was making a come-back. In one particular game Colin led by 40-owe 30 and Barry played magnificently to recover to 30-40 and then lay a chase of half a yard. As he came up to serve he whispered to those of us in the dedans, 'Let me know if it's coming in.' He then served and Colin crashed his return right into the top corner of the dedans to win a crucial game. Barry turned and slowly walked back to pick up the ball. 'I thought we had an agreement', he observed to us meaningfully, his eyes sparkling.

The Royal Melbourne Tennis Club was blossoming at that time. The work was hard, for we were up to one hundred and sixty hours of tennis booked per week, and the door bell and telephones used to ring incessantly, but the working conditions were good and the atmosphere excellent. Colin, Lachie and I had moulded into a good team and we had a lot of fun. We invented a score or so of games which we played around the club, all prefixed by the word 'Royal'. Royal Squash was played at the service end of a tennis court, using a lawn tennis ball, and was one of the simpler games. Royal Secret Service Agents was much more complex and involved up to twelve competitors creeping around the entire club in the middle of the night, each armed with deadly weapons (a squash ball and a water pistol) trying to liquidate each other and to find a hidden brief-case, which had to be taken to Tangiers (the club bar).

The most dangerous game of all was Royal Hockey, which has no rules, except that the idea is to score goals in the last gallery and the winning gallery, using tennis equipment. The injuries were horrifying, and Graham Hyland had to bar himself from playing for life, before he decapitated someone.

One night Lachie and I volunteered to alter the coloured trim on one of the courts from a rather insipid yellow to a pillar-box red. This entailed painting the grille, the bandeau and two of the lines on the floor. The bandeau proved the most troublesome, because it was an awkward height for painting and care had to be taken not to get paint on to the penthouse. 2 a.m. saw Lachie finishing off one of the lines on the floor, me halfway up a ladder attending to the bandeau, and Graham sitting on the penthouse chatting to us while we worked. I stepped off my ladder, on which was resting the paint-tin, in order to rest my arm. At that moment, without realising the possible consequences, Graham casually kicked the top of the ladder, so that it rose towards the vertical and then fell back against the penthouse. Cor blimey! What a mess! Pillar-box red all over the first gallery, the ledges, the wall and the floor - and my face, probably. In the middle of the night we had to go round knocking up the neighbours in search of supplies of turpentine.

Another great game was Royal Aquaplaning. Tennis courts make charming venues for dinner dances if between one hundred and twenty and one hundred and eighty people are involved. The setting is impressive and the galleries lend themselves naturally as serving hatches for buffets and refreshments. The only problem is that it usually makes one hell of a mess of the floor from drips of melted butter, cigarette butts and the like. The Royal Melbourne Tennis Club used to hold dinner dances annually on the South court and we, the staff, decided that the best way to clean up was by flooding the court in an inch or two of water and then scrubbing the affected parts as they were submerged. After this was done we used to spend some time belting around the court aquaplaning on our bare feet. This became known as such fun that, after a couple of years, we were getting volunteers to help clean up after dinners in return for an hour's splashing about afterwards.

My next trip overseas was in November 1977, and my first stop was at Queen's Club for the British Open. Seeded fourth, I injured my back when winning the quarter-final and had to scratch after a few games in the next round.

In most active sports there are a number of standard injuries, such as twisted ankles and torn ligaments around the knee joints, but tennis players have additional problems to cope with owing to the nature of the equipment used. The ball is just small enough to enter the eye socket and damage the eye. This usually occurs when a ball flies off the edge of the racket towards the face of the striker. It can happen at any standard and, although I don't wear them myself, protective sports eyewear should be considered. Should an injury occur then the victim should keep as still as possible and be transferred immediately to a specialist eye unit, as there may be a rupture of the retina. With the advent of lasers there is an excellent chance of repairing any such damage; but many eyes have been lost in the past and any accident of this sort must be attended to promptly.

131

The racket is a heavy implement and causes a number of cases of tennis elbow, wherein the tendons and/or ligaments become inflamed and painful. The cure is rest, or at least rest from the offending action. This may entail a visit to your local professional for advice on how to correct faulty stroking techniques and jarring movements. You should also ensure that your racket grip is not too small and consider having the racket re-strung in natural gut, as this causes less vibration in the arm than synthetic strings. Another remedy is to bind the wrist in such a way as to restrict its movements. I do this simply by wearing three sweat-bands on my wrist, all on top of each other. Thus restrained, the tendons that run from the shoulder to the fingers are not stretched to the full and the traumatisation of the affected area is reduced.

Back problems arise at tennis because of the bending and stooping involved, the sudden changes in direction and the rushing about on an unforgiving, solid floor. If you have a suspect back then prevention is far better than cure. Ensure that your footwear is good, inserting heel-pads if necessary, moderate your contortions during the first few minutes of play, and seek advice on what exercises you can do to protect your back. As a result of my own injury, I now do about ten minutes of selected isometric exercises each day. These are simple and relatively painless and they improve the muscles that run alongside the spine, which are then capable of increased spinal protection. In my opinion, unless your family doctor is a sports injury specialist, persistent trouble should always be treated by a well-qualified osteopath. I see an osteopath about twice a year, purely as a prophylactic measure: in my job I can't afford to have a couple of months out of action.

As far as legs go, the best advice is to develop the habit of doing a few loosening movements before you take to the court. Bounce up and down on your toes, do a few deep knee squats, and stretch your hamstrings by standing three feet from and facing a wall and then leaning gently towards it, with your arms as brakes, while keeping your heels on the ground.

Now I am no doctor or physiotherapist. All of the above concerning injuries should be regarded as tips from an experienced lay-man. If in doubt you should consult a specialist.

From Britain I flew to America for the 1978 U.S. Open, where I lost to Jimmy Burke in the semi-final. This was a good win for Jimmy, as I had beaten him in the final of the U.S. Professional Championship the week before. It was an important result for me, too, because it hurt badly and one always learns more from defeat than from victory. I had

Jimmy Burke

led by two sets to one, two games to love and 40-30 but then lost twelve games in a row, and the match.

The main reason was the volleyed return of serve which Jimmy had and I did not have. Until then, I had always returned serve after the bounce and that policy had never let me down. Now I found myself facing an opponent who concentrated entirely on length for his service and who was capable of trickling the ball along the penthouse with no spin whatsoever, so that it finished deep in the forehand corner at a very slow pace. It was a very difficult service to attack with my methods and I wasn't up to the job. Meanwhile, when I was serving, Jimmy was taking the vast majority of my deliveries on the volley. He did this by nimbly positioning himself under the ball as it approached, crouching down and striking it about head high with a lot of sidespin. It was not a devastating shot, but a very consistent one, curling at medium pace into the forehand corner where the sidespin would take its effect. It was, in fact, just the sort of return I needed to counter Jimmy's own services. And there I was: the initiative taken away from me at both ends of the court.

Jimmy is a fine player, but in a defensive sort of way. His mobility is extraordinary and he scurries about the court retrieving seemingly

133

impossible shots. There is nothing dynamic about his attacking strokes, for he eschews cut and pace in favour of line and length, prepared to prolong the rest until his opponent makes an error. His judgment of balls hitting or missing the tambour is outstanding and he doesn't have any obvious weaknesses. The secret of tackling this type of player is controlled aggression. Unless your natural game is all-out attack, then you are liable to become wild and make too many mistakes if you go flat out. On the other hand, if you try rallying with him you are playing into his hands and you will surely lose. So play your own game, but with just ten per cent more bite to it and trust that your remorseless, steady attack will wear him down spiritually, so that he feels an inferior player.

For myself, I determined to learn how to play the return of serve on the volley. This was achieved, in training, by throwing hundreds of balls on to the service penthouse and volleying them as they bounced off. The fundamentals to learn were (a) good footwork and balance (b) to keep my head still during the stroke - which reduced errors dramatically and (c) to make the stroke short and crisp.

The next step in training was to take a basket of balls to the backhand side of the dedans and strike them one by one off the main wall, so that they bounced back towards me along the dedans penthouse. This makes an excellent simulated service which can be volleyed at a target that should be chalked faintly on the main wall, at head height above chase three and four.

The last, and best, method of acquiring this stroke is to sacrifice your results for a few weeks or months and to attempt to play every serve you receive on the volley. You will soon learn what is easy, what is possible, what is inadvisable and what is out of the question. What I found was that the easiest balls were those which were rolling along the penthouse and those which took only one or two bounces. This was doubly useful because it showed me that I should attempt, when opposed to a committed volleyer, to make my own services take about four scudding hops.

The time had come for the Ronaldsons to leave the Royal Melbourne Tennis Club. It was going through a period of consolidation, rather than one of expansion, which was less stimulating and, with Barry Toates now living in America, Australia had become even more isolated in terms of competition. It was very expensive making long trips abroad in search of tournaments and experience.

It is ironic that a successful professional often finds that his influence at a club actually diminishes as years go by. If I may define myself as successful, at least in terms of increasing membership and court usage, then this has beset me on more than one occasion. What happens is that when a new pro arrives at a struggling club and starts to get the wheels turning, the existing club committee (which has known hardship) is terribly grateful to him, heeds his every suggestion, and allows him a free hand in the day-to-day running of the club. Time passes, the club expands and soon new faces start to appear on the committee. Having never known the club to be anything but successful, they assume that this is the norm and are, justifiably, less beholden to the pro. At the same time, the committee business moves away from simply struggling for survival and starts concentrating on pleasant but less fundamental issues. Quite rightly, sub-committees are set up to deal with these matters and efficiency improves. The tournament schedule is altered, social functions are arranged, waiting lists for membership are formed, and five-year plans for maintenance are drawn up. All this is wonderful for the club, and therefore for tennis, but it can be sobering for a professional who finds that he is now only consulted on specialist matters, and who undergoes a dramatic devolution of influence. Character-forming, that's what it is.

I was required to give six months notice of leaving Melbourne and, after I had done this, I set about finding a position in the Northern Hemisphere. I wrote to half a dozen clubs that seemed to be in need of a professional and, from the three that responded, Lesley and I selected Troon in Scotland. Despite apologetically offering only the most meagre remuneration, it was the sheer enthusiasm of the letters we received from Alastair Breckenridge and Iain Tulloch that clinched it for us.

I served those last few months at the R.M.T.C. under the presidency of Colin Gurney, who had succeeded George Limb. It was Colin who had supervised the construction of the new club premises, and he was also responsible for the introduction of the sub-committee system that worked so well at Melbourne. The Gurney style of leadership did not appear dynamic, but rather consisted of quietly arranging around himself the men who would efficiently carry out the committee duties and, ultimately, take over from him. Personally, I was afraid that the Royal Melbourne Tennis Club was trying to become a leading light in the arena of posh Melbourne establishments, rather than a star in the world tennis firmament; but these fears seem ill-founded, as it has probably achieved both aims.

135

CHAPTER 21

TROON

In November 1978 we packed our trunks and returned to Britain. First stop was the British Open at Queen's - and here I won my first really important tournament by defeating Peter Dawes, Alan Lovell, Norwood Cripps and, in the final, Howard Angus, the world champion. Because I was the underdog, and because it was desperately close, that final was my most memorable match. I led by two sets to love, was caught at two sets all, and eventually recovered to win from 4-3 and 40-love down in the final set. Incidentally, I thus became the first player to win this tournament, whose surname did not end in 's'. Previous winners were Ron Hughes, Frank Willis, Howard Angus, Norwood Cripps and Chris Ennis.

It was a timely boost for me in that, a fortnight later, I was due to play Norwood Cripps in an eliminator for the World Championship. This was held at Hampton Court and, by dint of an effective giraffe service combined with the old pass rule, I ran out the winner by five sets to one. In those days, a service which was otherwise good but which landed in the area in front of the grille was called a pass everywhere except in America, and was counted as a let. This meant that you could serve deep giraffes which were repeatedly lets, until one fell on a perfect length. As long as you had control of this difficult service and projected it long, rather than short, then you were in the driving seat.

We moved to Troon and immediately struck the worst winter for sixteen years. Many were the days that I had to sweep the snow off the court after it had been driven through the eaves in the roof; and many were the times that I rushed on to court as the players changed ends, in order to mop up the drips from the roof, which leaked chronically. Alastair and Jill Breckenridge had taken over the Sun Court Hotel in Troon in 1967. It had been built in the first decade of this century as the summer residence of Mr J.O.M. Clark, and there was a tennis court attached, although it had been out of use for many years. During the Second World War the Royal Navy had installed a large gun in the court, removing the side penthouse and side galleries as they did so. Later on, the dedans had been bricked up and the dedans interior had been used as bedrooms. With typical zeal, Alastair and Jill set about restoring the court. They were aided by a few tennis enthusiasts from up and down the country, who came along and splashed paint about in working parties; and in 1969 the court was re-opened for use.

Lesley Ronaldson

The Sun Court Tennis Club was formed with the blessing of the Breckenridges, who made no charge for the use of the court. A number of worthies joined but play was sporadic. Two junior professionals had a go at making a living there, but both gave up within months. During 1978 an average of six hours of tennis were played per week and some of those were in inter-club matches, so there was considerable scepticism regarding our chances of success when we arrived. Fortunately for us, the enthusiasm of the Breckenridges and some of the more fanatical members got us off to a good start. Les and I joined the local squash and lawn tennis clubs in order to develop contacts and, once the ball had started rolling, people were falling over themselves to take up the game. Tennis became quite a fashionable sport in Troon. Inside three months we broke seventy hours a week for the first time and our best week came in July, normally considered off-season, when we had eighty-eight hours booked.

In terms of breathing life into ailing clubs, I have an enormous advantage in that my wife is just as dedicated to tennis as I am, and is far more extrovert with it. She is particularly adept at persuading members that they should play three times a week, rather than once and that they should encourage their wives to play as well. She is a pretty mean performer herself and, that year, she won the first of her British Ladies Championships.

In April of 1979 I returned to London to continue my challenge for the World Championship. Jimmy Burke had emerged the victor from his eliminator with Gene Scott, and so Jimmy and I had to play a final eliminator for the right to challenge Howard Angus for his World Championship. Jimmy tried hard and ran like a rabbit, but I had learned my lesson well and discovered that his flat services were easy to take if you volleyed them.

A fortnight later Howard and I did battle. It was a massacre. On the first day I reached four games all in each of the four sets we contested, and every time Howard started peppering the grille at this stage. The point was not lost on me. If a set gets tight then find a way to maintain the service end; and don't just aim for the grille: hit it. A lot of matches appear to hinge on the ability to score with grilles at critical times, so practise hitting it until you expect to succeed. Howard won by seven sets to love, the second day more easily than the first.

I traipsed back to Troon with my tail between my legs, determined to include more forcing into my preparations for the forthcoming British Professional Championships at Leamington. Frank Willis was the defending champion, having held the title for the previous thirteen years on a challenge basis, but he had quit his job at the Manchester club in favour of squash, and I was the top seed for the event as he had hardly played for a year.

In the final Frank led me by five games to three but then lost twelve points in a row to lose the set. 'You're slipping, Frank', I thought to myself. In the second set he led 5-4 and 40-love, and seemed about to squander that advantage at 30-40 attacking chase worse than two, but he found a good stroke and took the set. I wasn't worried. His legs were

Frank Willis

six years older than mine and a long match didn't bother me. The score pottered along to 2-all in the third set when suddenly, at deuce in the next game, Frank won the match with a single stroke. I had forced high for the dedans and the ball dropped at about chase three on his backhand side, whereupon he crashed it into the nick in front of the tambour. It was by far the best stroke of the match, and it remains the best shot I have ever seen, but it took several seconds for the applause to come from the dedans. Like the marker, who was struck dumb and me, the spectators had been temporarily stunned. It just didn't seem possible to strike the ball so hard and with so much cut to such a position, but it happened. Frank had little trouble reeling off the games he needed for the match after that.

Frank is recognised as the most correct striker of the ball in modern times. All his shots are cut and most of them carry weight as well. It is alleged that as a lad, working at the Manchester Club, he used to nip on court after each match and cut three or four balls over the net while the next pair were spinning for service. He practised so much that the only stroke he knew was a correct one and, as a result, he hardly ever played an ugly or improvised stroke. Most players, when under pressure, are happy to return the ball anywhere as long as it goes over the net, but Frank usually manages to put the ball on the floor even when in dire straits. For some reason he has rather neglected his serving over the years and this has always been his Achilles heel, not that many are capable of exploiting it.

Frank is also one of the great humourists of the tennis court and his infectious laugh and cheeky asides make him the most watchable of players. He causes considerable merriment by the state in which he arrives for some of his matches. 'Am I really playin' now?' he protests. 'I can't play now. I can't even see straight yet. Who'm I playin' anyway? Am I playin' you, David? David, can *you* see the balls, can you?'

Back at Troon I took on an assistant to help me cope with the burgeoning Scottish game. Walter Gregg was then twenty-nine, Irish, and a very good all-round sportsman. He had been a teacher at a sports and leisure complex, could turn his hand to most games, and had represented his country at basketball. He very quickly picked up the basics of how to coach and play and, being mature, was fully conversant with all the skills required for running a club within a matter of weeks. In all, Les and I spent only ten and a half months in Troon before leaving Walter in charge and heading south for the vacant job at

Hampton Court. For the short time that we were together Walter and I had great fun. Like most Irishmen, he can talk the hind leg off a donkey and we ragged each other endlessly. You could always tell when you had really upset him because his lower lip would start to protrude. A half-lip wasn't all that serious, but a full lip meant an impending sulk.

I had had a poor year in tournaments, losing to Howard Angus in the World Championship Challenge, Frank Willis in the British Pro and Barry Toates in the Australian Open. Now I was to suffer an even more devastating reversal, while attempting to defend my British Open title. In the final of this important event Howard thrashed me ignominiously by 6-2, 6-1, 6-1.

At his best, Howard was the finest player I ever saw. In this match I attempted to keep the ball short in the hope that he would lift his head and overhit. In retrospect I can see that, with his lightning speed about the court and marvellous control of the racket face, this tactic was doomed to failure. Graham Hyland also tried to play Howard that way once, led by three games to two and then lost fourteen of the next sixteen games.

Strangely enough, I believe that Howard would have been even better if he had adopted different tactics. His only weakness is on the volley and yet, in important matches, he serves his railroad almost exclusively, thereby encouraging his opponent to force. If the going gets tough then he believes in pressure, and he applies this pressure by hitting the ball firmly about the court to keep the opposition at full stretch - and this again invites the force to his suspect volley. With five years as world champion, ten years as British Open champion and sixteen years as British Amateur champion to his credit, plus a string of similar successes at rackets, Howard's record is exceptional: but I am convinced that, had he learned an accurate giraffe or drop service, and maybe a slow drag service, and concentrated on making his opponents play their shots off the floor, then his margin of superiority would have been even greater. And if he so desires it would not be too late now.

Howard always maintains that his technique at tennis is poor. Modesty may have something to do with it, but it is nonsense all the same. His footwork is exemplary and his backhand is a model stroke, especially when chipping returns of serve. His rolled forehand is unorthodox, but it is still produced with sound balance and footwork and he still hits through the path of the ball. His relative weakness on the volley is because his natural volleying stroke is a cut one that comes across the line of the ball. Had he started playing in an era when the volley was as

Howard Angus

important as it is today then, obviously, he would have developed and strengthened this department of his game also.

CHAPTER 22

HAMPTON COURT

I started work at Hampton Court on the 19th November 1979, alongside Rob Bartlett, who began on the same day. I had known Rob since my Melbourne days when, as a farmer, he used to play in the same lawn tennis team that I did. We Ronaldsons used to spend our domestic holidays getting fat on his sheep farm. In 1978 he sold up and went overseas to see the world. By several strokes of bad luck he wound up sharing a room twelve foot by eight foot with both Lachlan Deuchar and Graham Hyland in Earls Court, London.

Now Lachie and Graham are hardly noted for decorous behaviour, but even they were taken aback by some of Rob's antics. Rob had a job at Heathrow Airport pushing trolleys about at six in the morning, so he had to go to bed early. The other two would usually come bounding in some time after midnight, boisterously waking him up as they prepared to retire. Half an hour after the light was finally turned off there would suddenly be a series of crashes against the wall. This was Rob hurling books at the light switch until it came on. Once woken, Rob was determined that no one else should rest. The others would be treated to a recital of Australian drinking songs, and lengthy exhibitions of rowing in bed, trampolining on the bed, and golf using a racket for a club, a roll of paper as a ball and Lachie's head as a tee. Graham learned to read in bed, with a retaliatory shoe raised above his head; and Lachie acquired the habit of hiding in the cupboard and reading with the aid of a shaft of light through the hinge. The mess was indescribable, for the entire belongings of those three scruffy Aussies were scattered untidily around that tiny room.

Once he had had enough of pushing trolleys around airports, Rob started to drive excursion coaches all over Europe for a living. After an eventful summer, that included several escapades best forgotten, he asked me if he could learn the trade of a tennis professional. The Tennis and Rackets Association's Young Professionals Fund came up with a grant, as they had for Walter Gregg, the Royal Tennis Court at Hampton Court acquiesced, and the deed was done. The Young Professionals Fund, founded by the late Dick Bridgeman some twenty-five years ago, has made a major contribution to tennis in this fashion. Rob's training period lasted only twenty weeks, during which time he proved himself a solid, conscientious worker and then he went to Canford School, where he started a new club from scratch and filled the vital role of instructing Canford boys on the intricacies of the game.

After that dismal year of competition outings, the 'eighties brought me a change of fortune. In 1980 I was undefeated and I attributed this to a number of factors. Firstly, my preparation for a tournament was more specific, and used to finish with a three-week plan that ran successively through various aspects of technique arranged like an elongated check-list.

Tactically, I had developed a disguised force and this is essential for the experienced player. My strategy, when receiving serve, is to play two shots out of three with cut into the backhand corner, and the third a force underneath the forehand corner of the dedans. My opponent is then required to cover balls at chase a yard in the backhand corner and better than second gallery on the forehand side. This diagonal stretches him far more than an ordinary floor game that demands covering only the width of the court. There are side benefits too, most notably that a number of forces will fly a little too high and give me an outright winner in the dedans.

Nowadays many competitors employ the same tactic, and some apply it in reverse by attacking the forehand corner on the floor and the backhand corner of the dedans. As a general rule I think this method is slightly inferior. Most players are better at digging balls out of the forehand, rather than the backhand corner and, all too often, even defensive shots will float into the grille or fly off an edge of the tambour when hit from the forehand. In addition, should the force miss the backhand side of the dedans then it will rebound into the court well away from the side wall, whereas my force to the forehand side tends to hug the main wall.

The third reason for my new-found success was my advancing reputation as a tough competitor - one who won more than his share of 6-5 sets and fifth-set matches. At any level of the game a good match temperament is essential. Even in a low-grade club tournament, the winner will be one with a steady hand and some steel in his mind, for unless you are miles better than the other contestants you are unlikely to go through successive rounds of a tournament without facing the occasional crisis.

Sportsmen are inclined to have double standards in their attitudes to their games. A squash player with a lousy backhand and poor match temperament will practise his backhand for hours on end, but merely shrug his shoulders about the mental problem. The ability to win tight contests can be developed, but it takes time and training like anything else. Essential to this is a positive attitude. Avoid the sinking feeling when your opponent catches up to five games all. Develop an appetite for the scrap, win or lose. Don't complain about your luck, either inwardly or vocally. Some players become desperately wild when it comes to the crunch, while others are overtaken by nervous timidity. Try to think of controlled aggression, firm and positive - and retain the service end as much as possible. Do not leave a ball that you fear you might mess up, in the hope that you can beat the chase at the other end; keep your head down and hit it firmly for the tambour instead.

Luck is a funny business and I don't really believe in it or its capacity to swing matches. A service which nicks is a good service, not a lucky one, because that is what the server intended and, in any case, his opponent could have volleyed it had he read it correctly. After thirteen years of watching matches I have been astounded by the manner in which fortune almost invariably favours the player who is in the ascendancy anyway. This being so, 'luck' is predictable and, if it is predictable, then it is not luck in the first place. All you have to do is to start winning on your own merits, and suddenly Lady Luck will leap onto your bandwagon and start finding all sorts of dastardly bounces on your behalf.

A player who is three games to five down sees his opponent's shot bounce off the grille penthouse and fall vertically down the grille wall. 'Oh no!' he sighs, 'Not again! That's the fourth one of those today.' Should the same thing happen to his opponent the latter will recognise a challenge, move his feet and have a go at it. Even if he fails, he will forget the incident immediately and get back to the business of rubbing Old Moaner's nose in the dirt.

The British Professional Championship of 1980 was held at Moreton Morrell and was the most exciting tournament of the year. Barry Toates had saved match points in his quarter-final win over Kevin Sheldon and next faced Frank Willis in the semi. This turned out to be a classic match, with each receiver making the server rush from corner to corner in beautiful, protracted rallies on the floor. Barry forced a fifth set by staging a come-back from two games to five down in the fourth, which rather flattened the champagne which had been prematurely opened by the sponsor in recognition of a great match. In the end Frank won the fifth set by six games to three.

In the other semi-final Graham Hyland made repeated recoveries against me, before losing at the last gasp in the eleventh game of the final set. Graham was then working at the New York Racquet and Tennis Club and was showing notable improvement in his volleying of the return of serve. He had demolished Norwood Cripps in the previous round making much use of this stroke.

The final was just as much a cliffhanger. Having scampered about for over three hours against Barry the day before, Frank was to do the same against me, grunting as he dug into the corners and characteristically chewing his tongue as he served. Eventually Frank reached 5-3 in the fifth set, but I prised the next two games away from him and saved two match balls in the final game, before winning the match by beating chase worse than a yard on the floor on my sixth match point. The score was 6-4, 4-6, 5-6, 6-4, 6-5.

As if that wasn't enough, the final of the Taylor Cup for young professionals was also decided in the last game of the final set. Walter Gregg emerged the winner and Jonathan Howell the plucky loser.

At the Royal Tennis Court, bookings were running three times as high as in the previous year and my application for a new assistant was granted. The lucky lad was Alistair Curley, who was one of the new members at Troon. He came to join us despite howls of protest from his mother, who could not understand why he did not want a 'proper' job. The 'Commandant' as Alistair used to call her, is quite a personality. Worried about him being cold in the draughty palace, she would send him letters counselling cups of hot soup before bedtime and reminding him to keep his back cosy. When he subsequently moved to Hobart she was mortified by the Tasmanian twang that he picked up.

Alistair became an efficient professional in no time at all, being competent at everything he did except wagering and coffee competitions. He was so bad at making bets that you were well advised to accept any wager he offered, even if the facts were unknown to you, on the grounds that he was likely to be wrong anyway. The coffee competition is a silly game played to decide who makes the coffee. Balls are thrown around a course towards a target, but Alistair was hopelessly handicapped because he never knew which hand to throw with and, in any case, he couldn't hit the floor with his hat.

On the subject of hats, it was about now that Lesley completed her hat-trick of boys. Luke appeared in October 1980, to make up our men's doubles game. Lesley and I both suffer from enormous parental pride and I can't put into words how much pleasure these chaps have given us. All my assistants have always had to be surrogate uncles, nannies, nappy-changers and baby-sitters and all appear to have become genuinely attached to the children.

The national sponsor in Britain was then Unigate, a big improvement on their predecessors in that the support was more extensive in terms of events covered, as well as more generous. I had beaten Howard Angus twice that year already, including the final match of the special world event arranged by Unigate, but I was still anxious to gain my revenge in the British Open for the drubbing he had given me the previous year. It was not to be. A week before the tournament started, Howard was struck a glancing blow in the eye by a rackets ball and he had to scratch. Although Howard was said to have made, eventually, a complete recovery from the injury, he was never quite the same force again and his self-confidence certainly suffered.

I finished the year by defeating Frank Willis in an eliminator for the World Championship Challenge that was to take place the following Easter, and started 1981 with a trip across the Atlantic to defend my U.S. Open Singles title in New York. It was here that, after years of promise, Graham Hyland finally came good and won the event. Not only was his play superior, but he won his last two matches in the fifth set as well, thereby demonstrating an improved match temperament. True to form, just when he appeared to have found the formula for success and was set to take the world by storm, he suddenly quit the game and returned to his parents' farm near Hobart.

I lost to Graham in the semi-final of that U.S. Open. The round before I had had a narrow escape before defeating Wayne Davies in five sets, and it was Wayne who was my opponent in the final of the U.S. Professional Championships at Tuxedo the next week. This was a tremendous tournament for him because, even though he lost to me again, he had defeated both Barry Toates and Jimmy Burke in previous rounds - and this after only two years as a professional.

Wayne was assistant professional to Lachlan Deuchar in Hobart at the time and, for mutual experience, a swap had been arranged for the two assistants so that Alistair Curley would go to Hobart and Wayne would travel to Britain. This was most beneficial to me as Alistair was not yet of a standard to extend me, whereas Wayne would be able to assist my training for the World Championship.

Wayne has a voracious appetite for practice and an inquisitive sporting mind. He is unimpressed by traditional techniques for their own sake and is always on the lookout for effective innovations. In addition, he examines the styles of other leading players and tries to copy their best strokes, even if they are unorthodox. Being a good student of the game, talented and an assiduous trainer, he was bound to succeed quickly.

Wayne's own game is notable for its consistency, for the severity with which he attacks any loose ball on his forehand, with both pace and cut, and for his punishing forehand volley. From the service end he strikes

Wayne Davies

this volley with great accuracy and penetration into the grille corner, using the full face of the racket. His most devastating stroke, however, is his volleyed return of serve, which he employs as often as he can. When awaiting the serve, Wayne grasps his racket with a square 'hammer' grip, slightly open, in order to ensure a locked wrist, and turns his shoulders away from the server. He allows the service to reach a point opposite him before striking at it, directing his blow towards the ball rather than across it and allowing the racket face to propel the ball cross-court with sidespin and cut. This shot moves quickly, swerves

148

violently away from the server into the main wall and cuts down sharply off the back wall. It is probably the single best stroke in world tennis today.

This pre-emptive strike policy is very effective and the only way to counter it is to find a service that is difficult to volley, without being a sitter off the back wall. If you can take away this initial weapon then the boy can be beaten - provided you work at it patiently. For the rest of his game, Wayne is very conscious of keeping low, using a firm wrist and following the line of the ball.

Away from the court, Wayne's two main hobbies are talking and one-upmanship. Talking he is good at, as long as you don't mind the subject always being tennis, for which he has boundless enthusiasm. As for the other: well, he must be the world's worst. Rather as in tennis, he goes for the early kill, leaping into a discussion with a bold assertion before he has had time to reflect on its wisdom. Once committed, he will stick to his guns to the bitter end as, step by step, his theory is painstakingly dissected and refuted. When all is lost he will break into a broad grin and quickly cast around for a new rock to bash his head against.

Wayne arrived at Hampton Court, with his wife Suzanne, just two months before the World Challenge was due and we practised long and hard together. This was mutually beneficial as it sharpened me up and it hauled Wayne into world class. The only Open tournament before the World Championship was the Scottish Open which, that year, boasted the strongest field I have come across. Howard Angus, the world champion, was drawn to play Wayne in the first round and the new U.S. Open champion, Graham Hyland, in the quarter-final. Howard was recovering only slowly from his eye injury and had lost the British Amateur Singles, for the first time in a decade and a half, to Alan Lovell a couple of weeks earlier. To his enormous credit Howard held off both Wayne and Graham before losing to Alan in the semi-final. In the other half of the draw Barry Toates surprisingly lost to Norwood Cripps, and I found myself in the enviable position of needing to beat Norwood and Alan to win the event, when both were near exhaustion after their previous conquests.

Barry had qualified as the U.S. challenger for the World Championship and he and I were due to contest the final eliminator, with the winner to challenge Howard. After our respective showings in Scotland, I had reason to believe that Barry would not present too much of a problem over the best of thirteen sets. In the event, it turned out to be an extremely tense affair, with neither of us producing our best form because of nerves. The first day ended at two sets all and the second at four sets all; but on the last day the decisive first three sets came my way fairly easily.

In today's context, the extended challenge match may look a little out of place, but ever since records have been kept it has been used to determine the Championship of the World. In the last decade both the British Open and the British Professional Championship have switched from being challenge events to knockout tournaments and, one day, the World Championship may follow suit, although this might be a pity, after what is now two hundred and forty odd years of tradition.

The object of any World Championship determination should be to ensure that the best player in the world wins the title, and that he should be pitted against his chief rival in the final match. The merit in the challenge system, apart from the continuity of tradition in a game steeped in that quality, is that it reduces the chances of a player unworthy of the title sneaking through to take it. The present guidelines governing the administration of the World Championship state that an aspirant must first win one of the four major national Opens, then defeat other challengers like himself in a series of elimination matches, and finally he must assail the defending champion over the best of thirteen sets. Should champion or challenger fall ill or sustain an injury before this final match then the contest is deferred so that, unless the disablement is a long-term one, the title cannot be won by default. All in all, this amounts to a rigorous test of quality and anyone who passes it is indeed a worthy champion.

Were the Championship to be decided by a knockout tournament there would be the risk that, in a bad year, the world's leading player might be unavailable at that particular time; a second highly-ranked player might be injured; and in the final, played over the best of five sets, the stronger of the two remaining competitors might play below form and lose to someone who didn't really deserve, at that stage, to attain the pinnacle of achievement in tennis.

The major drawback to the challenge method is that it is inclined to over-protect the champion. The fact that he has to play only one match is of little consequence, because that match will be his severest test in any case, and it is open to debate whether the eliminating matches played by the leading contender serve to sharpen him or have the effect of draining him. No, the real problem is that the champion has a large measure of control over the scheduling of the challenge. He has the choice of venue and the choice of dates. These advantages are not outrageous when applied with honour, for it is reasonable for the champion to select a court to his liking and a time of the year to suit his training. Human nature being what it is, however, there can be a tendency to choose a court solely because the contender loathes it, or arrange the match at an inconvenient time for the contender. Even if the champion does the decent thing, rumours may well spread to the contrary.

It is important that the World Championship should remain a truly international title, universally recognised and without the conflict that exists, for example, in boxing, where two bodies vie for administrative control and each has its own champion. The governing associations that exist in tennis - the Australian Royal Tennis Association, the Comité Français du Jeu de Courte Paume, the Tennis and Rackets Association and the United States Court Tennis Association - are all manned by people who have the best interests of the game at heart. There has been no corruption or subtle erosion of standards by commercial interests. The area of common ground that is consistent with maintaining the soul of tennis and yet moving with the times, can be sought unhurriedly and without the problems attendant with television, huge amounts of cash and special interest groups.

For myself, I am happy for the challenge system to continue for as long as the game is contested by men of integrity. If and when the day comes when we all sink to the levels obtaining in some other sports, the powers that exist in the game will have to fashion an alternative scheme. In these circumstances, tradition will have evaporated anyway.

A lesser failing of challenges is that one seldom achieves the highest standard of performances in this mode of contest. When a leading player enters a tournament he knows that, to be victorious, he must win about four matches against different players and, despite the stratification of the entry, he cannot be certain of the identities of his opponents in the latter stages. As a result, he trains positively, attempting to achieve his best form against a composite of his adversaries.

By contrast, for weeks in advance of a challenge match, the contestants have clear images of the battle that lies ahead. As with boxing and chess challenges, there can be clashes of character because of the personal nature of the competition. Much of the training is negative, sacrificing a good stroke to the opponent's strength for a lesser shot to his weakness. This in itself actually lowers the standard of play when the day comes and it couples with the effect of nerves, which are often present at a long-awaited contest, to produce a rather grim, excessively tactical match.

151

On Friday 17th April 1981 I challenged Howard Angus for his World Championship for a second time. Despite the closeness of the sets, the tennis was typically lack-lustre. Howard served his railroad monotonously, and I systematically bashed my return diagonally across the court towards the corner of the dedans, hammering away at his dicey volley. When we changed ends he regularly chipped his returns into the side galleries to regain service, and the game followed a rather staccato pattern with very few lengthy rests to grace it. I was delighted to win four sets to love, and pleased to have won each of the three sets that went to the deciding game, but there was little else of which to be proud.

Howard's confidence was obviously at rather a low ebb, and I had heard stories of some terrible thrashings that he had taken in practice, so I half-expected him to fold his hand quietly. I was completely wrong. On the second day he started with a set that was plucked from his best years and won it easily, 6-2. The next was my own best set of the Championship and we were both playing well in the seventh set when disaster struck.

Trailing three games to five, Howard bravely saved two set points and won the game, retaining the service side. At 15-all in the next game he served a double fault. The following railroad did not hug the gallery wall as usual and I blasted it hard, as a boasted force for the dedans off the main wall. Howard raced over to try to intercept the shot and, in mid-flight, realised that the ball was going to be wide of the dedans and rebounding into mid-court. Changing direction as quickly as possible he tried to get into position to play the ball, which was now chasing him up the court. It hit him as he twisted to avoid it and, in the same instant, he badly wrenched a muscle in a calf as a result of his contortions. Unaware of the gravity of the injury, I paced around at the other end, trying to keep my concentration for the impending set point; but after a minute of hobbling around painfully, Howard realised that the damage was not transient and he extended his hand graciously in defeat. Rather unsatisfactorily, in the end, I had won the Championship of the World that had been my goal for so long. Apart from the damage to his leg, which took several weeks to heal, Howard appeared to be relieved. He had held the title with distinction for five years, and sport had gradually been losing its place, in his list of priorities, to his expanding family and his business commitments.

Shortly afterwards Wayne Davies moved on to Bordeaux and Alistair Curley returned to Hampton Court. Alistair's game had improved enormously and he was now a fully-fledged professional, although he was still a soft touch for a wager. He had had a great time in Hobart and soon an arrangement was reached whereby Alistair would return there as senior professional, and Lachlan Deuchar would arrive at Hampton in an attempt to develop his undoubted talents. Just by coincidence (wink) this gave me another top-line practice partner and, after four months of Wayne, the benefits of this were not lost on me.

Lachie arrived in October 1981 and we got down to some serious training. In many ways he has a very similar build to myself - we have height, weight, reach and puny arms in common - so it was natural we should strive to develop a common technique. This in turn meant that we became very sensitive to minor changes in style, because we looked at each other as in a mirror.

The strokes to which we paid particular attention were the forehand off the back wall at the hazard end and all backhands on the floor. The latter were simple in theory and only required heaps of repetition. First we had to get the (imaginary) line between the feet parallel to our intended direction of stroke, then take a large final stride down that line and, above all, concentrate on striking the ball way in front of the leading foot. As tall men, it was particularly important for us to develop the big step in order to reduce our effective height. Once done, we had the advantage of weight over the shorter man, although he was better capable of eleventh-hour adjustments.

The forehand off the back wall at the hazard end demanded more thought. Unless the ball in question is very easy to take, the natural return of this shot is a sliced ball cross-court into the server's forehand corner, over the low part of the net. The trouble with this shot is that unless it is very good it is usually very bad, in that if the server can put his racket on the ball, he can usually attack it. Many leading players are very strong in this corner, and we considered it advisable only to play strokes there as an occasional surprise, or if there were no reasonable alternatives.

The strategy that we finally opted for was a mixture of short, sliced balls to the backhand corner and thunderous forces for the forehand side of the dedans. This came fairly naturally to me, as it was similar to my ideas about return of serve. A lot of thought went into the technique of forcing. Old-timers like Frank Willis would cut the ball a little, even on this shot, whereas many modern players were starting to go for the dedans with topspin.

Forcing for the dedans should be divided into two parts. There are some balls, particularly those which strike the grille wall first and then move rapidly towards the net, which are hard to attack in any way other than by forcing, and these should be struck at top speed. Frankly, if you can bring your opponent to the stage where his first concern is self-preservation, he is unlikely to provide much protection for the dedans with his volley, and even less likely to scamper after a ball that has missed low or wide. In no way do I mean to imply that you should aim at or anywhere near your opponent. Mentally pick a spot in the dedans about three feet from one edge and wind up so that there is no doubt about your intentions. If your pace and accuracy are good enough then there is no danger to your adversary and no danger from him.

I once found Wayne Davies stringing his racket so tautly that he was going red in the face from the exertion. When I asked why such tension was needed he replied that he wanted a gun. 'A gun?' I queried. 'Yes,' was the answer, 'You know - to fire bullets with!'

The other type of force is the masked one, wherein the striker signals his intention to play a floor shot by the nature of his racket action and stance and then, at the last moment, snaps the racket face closed and shoots for the dedans, at only about ninety per cent power in order to improve accuracy. If there is sufficient deception, the server will be moving the wrong way and is likely to be defeated.

Tennis is a demanding sport and average club players, as well as beginners, have quite enough on their plates in terms of techniques, tactics and reading the ball, without worrying about the frills of the game. For experienced players and leading competitors, however, a certain amount of subtlety is necessary. As an example, if you have a number of service variations to your name, try to arrange them so that you can deliver at least two of them from any one position on court. Thus you can deny your opponent the extra couple of seconds of notification about your intentions. This will not significantly increase the number of aces that you serve, because the receiver still has plenty of time to get into position, but nevertheless he would prefer the additional mental preparation, so why not make him do without it?

The best opportunity for deceiving your adversary is when you are returning serve, because that is usually when you are under the least pressure. Try to develop stroking techniques that give you two stroke options, right up to the last fraction of time. The masked force described above is a case in point. Another instance that comes to mind concerns the main wall boasted force. Having zipped a couple of these past your opponent into the dedans, you might expect him to be anticipating this shot the next time you shape up in the same way, in which case he would be completely wrong-footed if you played a more angled boast, with the same action, that struck the main wall on your side of the net and bounced a second time underneath the last gallery. Most importantly, if you are an advanced player, you should try to practise your normal cut return of serve so that the server cannot tell, by your preparations, stance or racket action, which of the two corners at his end you are attacking.

Lachie likes to divide a player's ability into three categories, namely as a ball-player, as an athlete and as a competitor, and he rates each of

Lachie Deuchar

these categories about equal in their composition of a tennis player. His ideal might be a cross between John McEnroe, Daley Thompson and Ron Barassi. By his own standards Lachie reckoned himself a fair ball-player, a good athlete and a mediocre competitor, and he set about improving the weak points.

Lachie quite fancies himself as a rager, and he can certainly be eccentric at times. Once he attended a party at Queen's Club, where he spent much time drinking triple whiskies and physically turning girls upside down. On his way out with some friends at about 2 a.m., he found himself confronted by a car moving slowly towards him along the drive. While his chums parted to allow the vehicle through, Lachie marched straight on, up, over and down the other side, leaving the driver bewildered and speechless.

Some little while later, he and I were due to contest the final of our squash club championships, and the club secretary was standing on the squash court, giving an introductory speech to the fifty or so spectators who had turned up to watch from the upstairs gallery. In the middle of his oration he glanced down to the court door where Lachie stood, unseen by anyone else, with his pants down and a big grin on his face. The poor secretary lost the thread of his speech completely and retired coughing and spluttering. However Lachie was his friend, and the secretary later confided to me that he wished he had dragged Lachie into the court as he was, just to wipe the smile off his face.

The old order in tennis was changing. The trio that had dominated the British scene for fifteen years were no longer around. Howard Angus had moved from London and was playing once a fortnight rather than three times a week, and both Frank Willis and Norwood Cripps were now employed as professionals at other racket sports. Although Gene Scott still regularly won the U.S. Amateur Championship, he, Ralph Howe and the Bostwick brothers, Pete and Jimmy, were no longer able to hold the top professionals over five sets. The new order consisted mainly of the quartet of Australian professionals: Graham Hyland, Colin Lumley, Lachlan Deuchar and Wayne Davies, plus the two British pros who had trained them: Barry Toates and myself. In addition there were Jimmy Burke from Philadelphia, David Johnson from Queen's Club and Alan Lovell, who was taking over as the world's leading amateur player.

The boomerang was becoming a very fashionable service. Some players were capable of serving it so accurately and monotonously that rumours abounded that it would have to be banned. The objection was that the boomerang could be learned in five minutes, and was threatening to

156

make extinct the time-honoured services that took months of practice to perfect. Many years earlier, the introduction of the American overhead railroad had sparked a similar outcry. As time passed, players had found ways of dealing with the railroad, and so Lachie and I set about researching methods of countering the boomerang.

A good boomerang, when it eventually leaves the side penthouse, runs parallel to the grille wall. If it is within two or three inches of that wall there is little you can do except applaud the server's touch. However, given just another three inches, you can make a positive return. Left-handers can move around the other side of the ball and play a forehand boast into the main wall. For the right-hander, we decided that both the lob and the boast on to the wall above the service penthouse were too defensive and admitted at least a moral defeat. The answer we came up with was a high, cut lob, struck from over the right shoulder with a lot of sidespin, and designed to arc high in the air before landing on the edge of the penthouse above the last gallery. Whether it lands on the penthouse or just misses it, the ball will kick violently towards the centre of the court and is a very tricky ball to take, negating most of the advantages gained by the good length boomerang. The other decision we made was to punish the bad boomerang as obviously and forcefully as possible, in order to dishearten the server.

In June 1982 Wayne Davies moved from Bordeaux to be head professional at the Racquet and Tennis Club in New York, thereby completing the remarkable achievement of having been employed as tennis professional in each of the four tennis-playing countries within the space of eighteen months. Unfortunately the reason why he left France so early was because the Jeu de Paume de Bordeaux had run out of money and was facing closure.

The Club at Bordeaux was a new one, for the Committee had followed the Melbourne example of selling an ageing, deteriorating building on a valuable site in the city centre and moving to a larger complex in one of the city suburbs, Merignac. They had been dogged by ill-luck from the start. Unlike Melbourne, they could not show a financial profit from the move because of the prevailing land prices, and much fund-raising had to be conducted. They also had to vacate the old premises before constructing the new club, leaving a fifteen-month hiatus. Then, only a month after the completion of the building, the charismatic Club President, Claude Quancard, died prematurely. This was an enormous blow to tennis as Claude had been a very popular local figure and highly respected within the game. Tragically, within a few months his right-hand man, Jacques Gallinou, died as well and the succeeding President,

Pierre Blanchot, was burdened with the Club's cash-flow worries and personal ill-health.

When the news spread that Jeu de Paume de Bordeaux was bankrupt and might well fold, I approached the Bordeaux Club and asked if I could have a go at running the show myself. It was envisaged that I should have a franchise to use the facilities, pay the incoming bills, and retain any profits.

It has been my pleasure to serve as professional under many great club leaders, and two outstanding examples are Jack Douay and Ronald Swash.

At the time of the crisis, Pierre Blanchot had fallen very sick and had been forced to stand down as Club President. The man who assumed the mantle in these most trying circumstances was Jack Douay, a vigorous and determined general. He and I had long discussions as to how we could effect a rescue of the Club, by operating the franchise and engaging a team of English-speaking professionals who would rotate between Hampton Court and Bordeaux. The French taxation laws eventually defeated this scheme, but Jack was sufficiently impressed by my conviction that success was possible to commit the Club to the adoption of my methods, engaging me as employment consultant, but taking the risks and gains for itself.

Ronald Swash is a great man because, as Chairman of the Committee of the Royal Tennis Court at Hampton Court, he had the vision to allow me to attempt to resuscitate the court in Bordeaux, the twentieth to be built in that city, and one of only two still in use in France, the birth-place of tennis. He was aware that, as a result of the venture, I might have to be away from Hampton Court for months at a time, and that the Royal Tennis Court could only be disadvantaged by this. Nevertheless, being a statesman rather than a politician, he persuaded his Committee that, for the sake of tennis generally, this was a course that should be encouraged. And they were broad-minded enough to agree.

Hastily a team of stalwarts was put together. Originally it consisted of my old chum, Rob Bartlett and his wife, Denise, Jonathan Howell and Thane Warburg. The Bartletts were only recently married and had a few months to kill before returning to Australia to live. Rob had served as professional at Canford for two and a half years with enormous success, starting up a new club from scratch and continuing the good work at the school. His place at Canford was taken by my brother, Steve, who had done his apprenticeship as professional at Oxford, and who was showing great promise. Jonathan was looking for a new job after four and a half successful years at Moreton Morrell and, having exhausted England's supply, he was also in search of fresh pastures full of women. Thane was a language student at Cambridge, spending a year in Aquitane as part of his course, and was the practical joker in the squad.

Although I employed a total of nineteen people to work in shifts in Bordeaux during the first year, and they all played their parts in turning the ship around, it was these four who bore the brunt of the load. With Jack Douay to advise them of the peculiarities of the Bordelais and offering invaluable moral support, Rob, Denise, Jonathan and Thane set about clearing up the debris in the club, mounting a publicity campaign, installing new membership and accounting systems, and generally altering the image of a Club with a poor reputation in the area. Rob and Denise could speak no French at all, so there were moments of farce and hilarity to punctuate the sweat and despair. The Committee gave support where it was necessary and, to everyone's delight, the Club managed to break even in its first year under the new regime. Since then Jeu de Paume de Bordeaux has made steady progress and now ranks as one of the leading clubs in the tennis world, with well-utilised squash and tennis courts, high membership, and a full complement of enthusiastic permanent staff.

I had received two challenges for the World Championship. Colin Lumley had qualified for a challenge by winning the Australian Open in 1980 and 1981, and Wayne Davies was accepted by virtue of winning the U.S. Open in 1982. In October 1982 Wayne defeated Colin in the final eliminator, and he and I were due to meet for the title a fortnight later. Twenty-four hours before the contest, Wayne was struck down with appendicitis and the match had to be postponed for four months.

Training for a World Championship Challenge is a nerve-racking business. As the most important match in tennis there is terrific tension involved and this was, without doubt, partly why Wayne succumbed to illness at the moment that he did. There is much running, exercising and training to be done in order to maximise physical conditioning. Then there is the worry about technique, form, niggling injuries and whether a 'peak' is being reached at the right time. Finally one has to contend with the personal nature of the battle, as decribed earlier.

One of Wayne's strokes that I was losing some sleep over was his volleyed return of serve to the dedans. Thinking over this problem, Lachie and I came to the conclusion that when this stroke was successful it usually scored in the backhand side of the dedans. A little research

159

soon showed why. After serving I had been taking up a position in the centre of the court at chase two. From where the volleying receiver stands, this leaves a far greater gap on the backhand side than on the forehand, and that gap is accentuated by the natural swing of the volleyed return from right to left as he looks at it. Therefore I had to learn to adopt a position a yard to the left of centre whenever Wayne appeared likely to attempt this shot. This is an example of the sort of training we undertake.

The challenge match was re-arranged for March 1983 in order to give Wayne time to recover completely. The odds were still heavily in my favour. I had won all seven of my previous contests against Wayne, the match was being played on my home court at Hampton and history was also on my side, in that only twice previously this century had a challenger defeated the holder at the first attempt.

We both played rather tentatively on the first day, which finished with the score at two sets all. On the second day I won all four sets and Wayne was limping badly by the end of play. Despite this, and needing to win all five sets on the final day for victory, Wayne played two brilliant sets that last day, before running out of steam and going down by four sets to seven overall.

It was interesting to note that in the heat of the moment both contestants played one particular stroke, even though neither had practised it. Whenever the server fired for the grille and missed on the inside, the receiver would unleash a backhand force cross-court for the backhand side of the dedans. After the event was over, Lachie and I decided that if we were going to play that shot in battle, we might as well practise it and do it properly.

What we discovered was that you could force efficiently on the backhand if you confined the stroke to those balls striking the back wall first, and at least three feet above the nick. The technique is to start with the racket low and the racket head dropped, take a large step down the line of the force with the right foot, swing through the ball with a little topspin, and finish with the racket high but the body low and balanced. We made heaps of errors when playing this stroke to begin with, but gradually it became an asset when used judiciously. In the server's mind it increases the penalty of aiming for the grille and missing. We found this backhand force particularly useful at doubles where, at the top level, physical strength on the main wall side of the player's body is one of the factors that separates the men from the boys.

160

Until this time my record at doubles had been dismal which, maybe, is why you will find little mention of doubles in the preceding pages. Now, armed with this new weapon, plus a new-found understanding that I was of more use on the backhand side when at the service end, even though this meant that I received only a small percentage of balls there, my doubles play began to pick up.

After years of battling together unsuccessfully, Mick Dean and I managed to win the British Open Doubles a couple of times. The key to success in doubles, I found, is the selection of strong partners. Mick had always been a good doubles player because of his solid volleys. On the international scene my partner is Barry Toates, one of the master tacticians at doubles. Barry has a wonderful sense of when to use the openings, particularly the winning gallery, and an aim to match. However his unique skill at doubles is his play from the forehand corner at the service end, whence he has the control to play the ball low and short to the base of the tambour, even when he is under pressure. This strategy seldom wins points outright, but very few players are capable of dealing positively with low balls around the tambour, with the result that many errors are forced and, more commonly, weak returns are induced for Barry to dispatch in his own artistic way.

The results of doubles matches are rather less predictable than those of singles, and surprises are more common. Certain players, such as Dinny Phipps, and Tony and Ted Cockram, are doubles specialists. They combine fierce driving with good counter-attacking volleys, keeping a fast pace going and making few mistakes. In general, players at the hazard end do not fare too badly as long as they can attack the ball. Once the initiative is lost, the hazard end players are unlikely to regain it. The boomerang is a very popular doubles service because it frequently takes away this initiative immediately and, even when the length is poor, it is difficult for the receiver to make a decisive strike.

In May 1983 Lachie and I were joined by Mike Gooding, an eighteen-year old Scot who came to Hampton Court for a crash course in the skills of the trade. Puds, as he is known, had been playing as an amateur at Troon for two years, and had been appointed professional there when a vacancy occurred. He survived the course, including Les' cooking and the bullying from my sons, and returned to Scotland after four months as a highly promising professional, with the considerable task of revitalising the Sun Court Tennis Club.

Tennis in Britain is now being sponsored by George Wimpey plc. They are pleased to be associated with a game that has maintained its standards of honour and sportsmanship. For all its faults, such as introversion and lingering snobbishness, tennis is still a game wherein officials are respected, behaviour is courteous, good shots are acknowledged by the opposition and traditions are observed, such as the custom for the incoming server to cross the net first.

Officiating at tennis is no easy matter. The rules are complex and the range of vision required is demanding. The best place for a single umpire to adjudicate from would be by the net at the main wall, but this is obviously impractical as he would interfere with play and expose himself to considerable danger.

In the Northern hemisphere, the marker stands by the net under the penthouse and suffers the disadvantages of being reliant upon sound for his determination of penthouse faults on service, and is poorly placed to see the short chases at the service end, in amongst the tangle of legs and flailing racket. In Australia, the marker sits in the forehand side of the dedans and has to rely on the receiver to call the hazard chases. The referee, if any, sits in the dedans (on the backhand side in Australia) and can be appealed to by either player on any matter of current play.

All too often markers are inclined to be a little weak. The players are normally separated by some twenty-five yards, and each has clear sight only of the chases at his end of the court. Therefore, if the marker is in any way uncertain about his call, he will tend to favour the player at the contentious end where the decision has to be made. A stroke off the tambour that might have been a winning shot or might have been a hazard chase, will sometimes be called as a hazard only because the server can't see it properly and the receiver might be upset if the ball were called good. A marker, like most ordinary people, will usually opt for the easy life.

Some competitors appeal to the referee on all possible occasions. I once saw a long rest in Britain that finished with the receiver setting chase better than two. The server swung round to the referee and appealed that one of his opponent's shots in mid-rest was 'not up'. On being turned down, he then suggested that his own railroad service had been a fault. When that was also refused he appealed for a chase correction and was awarded chase two instead of better than two.

To my mind this was iniquitous. Why should a referee sitting in the dedans be able to over-rule a marker on a question of 'not up', when the former is at least twice as far away from the scene? To be sure, the referee has a better view of the penthouse fault than the marker but, that being so, he should be responsible for calling the fault in the first place. One doesn't ask the square-leg umpire to give l.b.w. decisions at

162

cricket, with an appeal to the umpire at the bowler's end if one doesn't like the decision. And a minor alteration of the chase given only encourages players to keep appealing and saps the confidence of the marker.

Most sports have adjudicators whose decisions are final, and I believe that tennis would be better off that way too. If one seriously protests at the judgment of a referee at boxing, soccer or rugby, it will not alter the decision but only invite disciplinary measures. If a referee is consistently wrong then he will be removed as an official by the game's administrators. It should not be within the rights of the players to question an official. Look at the mess lawn tennis has got itself into by tolerating the remonstrations of players. It is a minority view at present, but I support those who believe that, at tennis, the referee should call faults on the penthouse and can only be appealed to on other matters by the marker himself, in the event of his being unsure or unsighted. Constant appeals by the players disturb the flow of a match and are insulting to the marker.

Even as things stand at present, I make it my policy never to appeal to a referee. This is not so much a form of altruism as a desire to put out of my mind any thought that my opponent may not have got that last ball up, or whatever the doubt may have been. Many players are guilty of playing out a rest half-heartedly, knowing that they will appeal at the end of it anyway if they lose it; and are then bitterly disappointed if the appeal fails. I believe that my confidence in the marker's decisions gives me greater opportunity to concentrate on my own problems rather than his. Of course, there are markers around in whom I have insufficient confidence, but it is preferable to request a different marker before the match starts, rather than to complain all the way through it.

In March 1984, Lachie defeated me in the semi-final of the Scottish Open. In its way it was quite a significant result. For Lachie it was proof that he had arrived in the top echelon of players; although he had trained long and well, and had achieved good results in practice, his tournament results had been disappointing. For me it was the end of a long run, in which I had been undefeated in singles for over three years and during which time I had won eighteen consecutive level singles tournaments.

Three months later I lost my first match to Wayne Davies as well, in the final of a World Invitation event, but it was a good year for me all the same because I managed to complete the Grand Slam of tennis: being holder of the British Open, French Open, U.S. Open and the Australian Open Singles Championships concurrently. Although this is

Group at Seacourt. Left to Right: Wayne Davies, Barry Toates, Lachie Deuchar, Peter Dawes, Chris Ronaldson.

164

a unique achievement to date, it has to be noted that some of these events have only been instituted recently, and so our forebears had no opportunity to attempt it. It is interesting that the same four countries which make up the Grand Slam at lawn tennis are the only four countries that have tennis courts in use today.

The most satisfying win in the Ronaldson family in 1984 was, however, young Ivan's victory in the British Under 12 Championships. It is another example of how far tennis has moved recently. These tiny players, who have to hoist themselves up on to the dedans ledge in order to reach a ball to serve with, display remarkable proficiency and clearly love playing the game. The standard of play, in this and in the Under 14, Under 16 and Under 18 events, was most impressive.

Techniques in tennis are constantly evolving. Certain strokes and tactics become fashionable for a period, until a successful counter is unearthed. Then they fade away and lie dormant for a few years, before surfacing again to cause fresh ripples of concern. Ten years ago the sidewall service was the most popular, until receivers began to hammer it on the volley. Then the emphasis switched towards railroads, until they began to be punished with forces. Nowadays the boomerang is all the rage, but in five years time .... who knows? A good player needs to have a wide-ranging armoury in order to get one of the early, comfortable seats on the band-wagon.

Just recently I have been working on what I call a 'second prize' concept. The idea is to play a tactical game based on strokes which are not too bad even if they don't go exactly as planned. For example, a straight force for the grille from the forehand corner that goes underneath its target is still a hard shot to counter-attack, whereas a boasted force from the same place will, if it misses low, present a much more friendly angle to the opponent. The former is clearly preferable for the server. At most levels of the game, the one shot that has no second prize is the cut or length shot to the server's forehand corner. If it is a good stroke then all is fine, but if it is imperfect it really is a shocker.

For a competitor, hard work is a vital partner to talent, technique and experience. Without it you simply cannot reach the limits of your potential. Late at night Howard Angus used to train by himself at Queen's Club, striving for perfection with his railroad and forcing. For ages I practised harder than anyone else around and many years later I reaped the reward. Today the three players who train the most seriously are the leading exponents of the game in the world. Tennis is truly an amateur game, for even the professionals play more for the enjoyment and companionship than for any financial gain.

A typical professional works long hours for a relatively meagre pay packet, especially in Britain. Despite this, it is a wonderful job for those temperamentally suited to it. Although the day is long, it is seldom arduous either physically or mentally. There is variety in the tasks to be performed, and the time is punctuated by contacts with club members who are almost invariably colourful, cheerful and friendly. The amateurs who play tennis are interesting people who are intrigued by a fascinating game. Because of the rapport that exists between them and the local pro, the latter always feels that he has access to specialists should an emergency arise. This can range from legal advice and medical attention down to lousy tips for the 2.30 race at Chepstow.

And then there are the humorous moments. Almost invariably there is a victim of the mirth. There is the junior professional who struggles for ten minutes (as I did) to put his first line of trebling in his first racket -normally a twenty second job - only to be told at the end that he has done it upside down.

Beginners often cause a few smiles, especially if they are clueless about ball games to start with. One such worthy came to me for coaching many years ago, when I was still at Oxford. I gave him an appalling lesson, seemingly unable to teach him anything as I rolled basket after basket of balls off the service penthouse. No matter what I said or how hard he tried, every ball evaded his frenetic swipes and bounced harmlessly between his legs. There was no question of collecting up the balls from the net at the end of each basket - they were all grouped together by the tambour. Acutely embarrassed, I asked Mick Dean, who was then my assistant, to give the gentleman his next lesson. Mick determined not to fall into the same trap as I had and advised his pupil to learn the stroke by hitting balls out of his hand. After Mick's demonstration the novice had a go at it. He threw the first ball ten feet in the air, and missed it by eight. 'No, no,' said Mick. 'You only have to throw the ball up a couple of inches - a bit like a table tennis service'. This instruction was followed carefully, except that the beginner forgot to remove his left hand after releasing the ball and gave himself a hearty blow on the fingers. Most of us have been bouncing and bashing balls since childhood and it is difficult to appreciate that the minority, who have had nothing to do with balls until adulthood, have to go through the same elementary learning process that we did at an age when to make four unsuccessful grabs at an easy bouncing ball meant frustration, rather than ignominy.

A beginner's first lesson is usually a pretty standard affair, as the instructor runs through his patter about the rules, the strokes and the basic tactics. In my own case I generally wind up the lesson with a gentle game, in order to give the pupil a feel for the flow of a rest. To add a little spice, I usually throw in a couple of sophisticated services by way of offering a glimpse of future treasures. Having delivered a gentle sidewall service that pushes him back towards the grille, I may let him have a railroad that goes the other way. I recall one particular novice who, on seeing the railroad for the first time, completely mis-read the spin and set off in the direction of the tambour at high speed. This alone was quite comical, but it is not all that uncommon. Most victims realise immediately that they got it all wrong and accept the incident in the spirit that it was intended. Not so our friend. Having arrived by the tambour, and with the ball a full thirty feet away underneath the winning gallery, he still took a hopeful swing at it. At times like these, it can be fairly difficult to keep a straight face.

I once marked a match in Melbourne between two newcomers to tennis. It was a handicap match and one of the contestants had been penalised quite severely on the grounds that he was a competent squash player. Overall the handicap was owe 30, receive $\frac{1}{2}$30. After warming up, the squash player lost the toss, hacked two returns of serve into the net, unwittingly set chase first gallery and changed ends to serve, taking up a position in the middle of the court at chase five. '40 - owe 30, chase first gallery,' I called. He hammered the ball into the door gallery 'One fault'. His second service cannoned off the service wall above the penthouse at seventy miles per hour. 'Double fault, game, the first game,' I intoned. 'The next game is an owe 30 - 30 game'. Having taken only one lesson, and being distinctly hazy about the rules, the server asked what he had done wrong. I explained that the ball was required to touch the service penthouse. From the same position he then blasted a series of faults, becoming more and more anguished with his failures, serving faster and faster, and with greater frequency. Every ball was too low, too high or too short on the penthouse. Sitting in the dedans, like all Australian markers, I was hard-pressed to keep up with him as I called the score. 'One fault, double fault, 40 - owe 30, one fault, double fault, game, two games to love, owe 30-15 game, fault ...' Down at the hazard end, the bemused opponent wasn't even watching the performance. He was completely occupied with scooping all the loose balls into the net. Not until we were in the second game of the second set, after seventeen successive double faults, was another service put into play.

Different folks have different attitudes to adversity. Most contain their feelings, and unfortunately some demean themselves by sulking, swearing or being abusive. It is left to just a chosen few to be genuine entertainers when fate strikes them one in the eye. One of the members of the Royal Tennis Court is just such a star. When things go wrong for him he paces about breathing deeply and deliberately, with murder in his eyes. Or else he might jump up and down in annoyance, and occasionally club himself with his racket. Once he became so frustrated with his efforts that he punched his racket repeatedly until he broke the strings in it. It didn't do much for his fist either. His best effort came one day when he missed a ball off the tambour completely. Having flung his racket down in disgust he found himself still enraged, so he hurled himself furiously into a side gallery. 'Where are you going?' asked his opponent. 'Oh, into hazard second,' he replied calmly, as he clambered out.

In March 1983 the Browning Cup, a handicap tournament for professionals, was held at Petworth. Lachie and I battled through to the final, and I won the toss and elected to serve. Just for the hell of it, I stood by the main wall and thumped my first service into the tambour so that it richochetted on to the service penthouse before dropping flush with the grille wall. Peter Dawes, who was marking, correctly called it a fault. Mischievously I appealed to the referee, who was the current English Amateur champion. Taken aback, he declared that he could see nothing wrong with the service, and instructed the marker to play a let. Lachie carefully shouldered his racket and very deliberately marched towards the dedans, where sat the referee. 'I beg your pardon?' he said solemnly. At this point the referee panicked and arbitrarily gave Lachie fifteen seconds to return to the hazard end in order to continue the match. This had no effect whatsoever on Lachie as he set himself, legs apart and arms akimbo, in front of the official. The situation was only resolved when I went down to the hazard end and Lachie served to me instead. To my knowledge, this is the only occasion when players have changed ends in mid-point, and without a chase.

And what of the future? Jeu de Paume in France is a question of survival, as it has a precarious base of only two centres. Mention has been made of re-opening courts at Versailles and Fontainebleau, but these are only possibilities. The British game has done well in the last decade, with increasing participation and the restoration of courts at Jesmond Dene in Newcastle and Fairlawn in Kent. It is slightly hamstrung by its administrative association with rackets, a sport in straits at least as dire, and by the way that the cost of playing has been repressed, which has inhibited possible commercial expansion, although the latter stricture has been eased of late. The U.S. too can report progress, as both Newport and Lakewood are back in use and there are high hopes for a revival in Chicago; but it is in Australia that momentum is at its greatest. The new court in Ballarat opened in March 1984, existing courts are packed to capacity, playing standards are improving, and every month another rumour goes round about the construction of some new court in one of the major cities. Not all of these come to fruition, but with three brand new courts up and running and another in Melbourne on the way, in addition to the well-established court in Hobart, the future looks bright in the Antipodes.

A club can barely exist without a professional, and I believe that the quality of professional drawn to tennis has a great deal to do with the health of the game. It is not so much his playing standard that matters, although that helps, but more his efficiency, dedication and above all his passion for tennis. Good professionals fill courts, make quality balls, develop fine amateur players and drum up enthusiasm within their clubs. It follows that to obtain this calibre of person one has to offer him an attractive package. This need not be anything sophisticated: simply a fair reward for his efforts, an identity within the game, and the opportunity to conduct his business with dignity. For a suitable person its a great job. And it's a great game. Let's hope it stays that way!

EPILOGUE

Wayne Davies' challenge for my World Championship in March 1985 was repulsed with some ease. Despite five-set matches against me in the British Open finals just before and soon after this challenge, both of which Wayne lost after holding handsome leads, the World Championship itself was rather one-sided. I won by seven sets to one, playing my best tennis on the second day to polish off the match.

Over the following two years, without being invincible, I remained well clear of my rivals, while Lachie Deuchar appeared to be overtaking Wayne in the pecking order. In 1986 I won six of the seven major singles events entered, losing only the final of the British Open, when I was handicapped by influenza. Lachie had ended a good year in which he had won his first national Open (the Australian) by coming back from two sets down to defeat Wayne in the British Open semi-final and then sorting me out in the last round. By contrast Wayne had a terrible year, winning absolutely nothing. My life-time score against him was 15 matches to 1 and it rather looked as if he might never get my measure. To cap all, he had to have the 1987 World Championship deferred by a few weeks in order to allow him time to recover from arthroscopic knee surgery.

Against this backdrop, Wayne's achievement in winning the game's highest honour, and especially at Queen's Club where his previous results were dismal, can hardly be over-stated. In the final eliminator against Lachie, the latter led by 6 sets to 4, the last two of which he had secured by 6/2, 6/0 and Wayne had shown great resilience in riding out that storm. He then wrested the title from me with a clever mixture of giraffe services, short backhands and accurate boasted forces off the main wall. He also won the lion's share of critical points. It was an heroic performance against the odds.

Wayne Davies held the title of World Champion of Tennis for seven years, during which time he saw off three challenges from Lachie Deuchar: in 1988, 1991 and 1993, before falling victim to the youth, vigour and skill of Rob Fahey in 1994. This is a distinguished record, especially when Wayne's numerous further knee operations are taken into account. The only gap in his list of achievements was his failure to win a British Open Singles Championship, after eight attempts in which he five times reached the final and twice stood at match and championship point.

This curiosity is an example of the recent trend of significant "home court advantage". Many of the world's leading men perform considerably better on certain courts as opposed to others: Julian Snow's run of three consecutive British Opens at Queen's followed on from Lachie's six successive victories, but most remarkable of all was Wayne's fifteen years without defeat at New York. Even in losing the World Championship to Rob Fahey (when he generously elected to cede the champion's right to defend at home only) he won the New York leg by 4 sets to 2.

Rob's accession to the title is notable on many counts. He was the first man since Jay Gould in 1914 to win the World's Championship at under the age of thirty; and the first since Norty Knox in 1959 to defeat the incumbent in his first challenge. Further, he has raised the level of enjoyment for spectators by his charisma and his style of play. His speed, agility and inventiveness of stroke are a joy to watch, especially in comparison with the era of slow serving and gallery play that preceded it.

From 1994, when he first won the World Championship, to 1999, Rob was clearly the best player in the world, but he had yet to assume a mantle of greatness, as he still lost some lesser matches through lack of preparation. From the turn of the millennium, however, he became an imposing colossus, raising standards to previously untouched peaks. There is no doubt in my mind that Robert Fahey is the best player who has ever lived. Most of the outstanding shots I have ever seen have been played by him and many of them were in the extraordinary first set of his title defence in Newport, Rhode Island, in 2004. Those of us who were lucky enough to be present regard that as the best set ever played because Tim Chisholm, a very worthy challenger who had only lost by 7 sets to 6 in his 2002 challenge, may well have played the set of his career and still lost it 6/2.

A major shake-up in the running of the World Championship took place in 2002, when the centuries-old tradition in which the champion selected the venue and timing for his next defence was abandoned in favour of a bid system. This means that instead of the title being contested for long periods in one country or even at one club, courts around the world are selected according to a set of criteria that includes the level of sponsorship, the playing quality of the court, the facilities offered (such as television coverage and spectator amenities) and an appreciation of when that country was last selected. Since its inception, Rob Fahey has successfully defended World Championship challenges at Hampton Court, Newport, Oratory and Fontainebleau, with Melbourne the venue selected for 2010.

By his own admission, Rob's best days as a competitor are behind him. The man most likely to succeed him is the diminutive Camden Riviere, who started playing the game in Aiken, South Carolina at the tender age of five! The differences between these players could hardly be more marked, as the most recent title match in Fontainebleau revealed. Rob was the powerhouse Australian, aged 40 and right-handed, who volleyed whenever possible. By contrast, the left-handed, ginger American challenger turned 21 on the first day of play and, appearing to be half his size, made much greater use of the back wall. Barring serious injury, Camden's day should come and, when it does, he may find that it is Steve Virgona who presents him with the most problems.

Rob's dominance has led to a scrutiny of his technique and tactics. He is very difficult to serve against because all services in the nick or shorter he volleys sharply down to chase a yard, while all deeper services are boasted off the main wall into the dedans at warp speed. Because his game is built on power, much of Rob's off-court training is centred on core strength and core stability. Naturally enough, many of the ambitious young professionals have copied his methods, with varying degrees of success. However, such is Rob's ability to hit the sweet spot even when playing extravagant shots, such as top-spin half-volleys off the main wall into the winning gallery, that I am reluctant to advise club players to 'try this at home'.

In recognition of the sudden growth of interest amongst women, a Ladies World Championship was inaugurated, as a biennial knock-out tournament, in 1985 and was first contested in Melbourne, where dear Lesley came within two points of winning the final. However, Judy Clarke triumphed to become the first champion and then retained the title at Seacourt in 1987. Since then, with the exception of 1993 when Sally Jones won in Bordeaux, Penny Lumley and Charlotte Cornwallis have cleaned up with six and four victories respectively. Sue Haswell and Jo Iddles, beautiful stylists and movers both, have graced the finals and won the doubles titles; and a new generation of stars are on the move, including Karen Hird and the Vigrass sisters, Sarah and Claire.

Court construction and renovation went through a boom period in the 1990s, but the flow has dried up in the new century, the only addition being Radley College, where I now ply my trade. Meanwhile courts have been lost at Greentree, Chelsea Harbour, Sydney and Romsey. My close friends have all suffered monologues from me on the necessity of creating a world-class venue for the sport. Ideally this would be a comfortable facility with at least four courts, preferably at a university close to a major urban centre. Such a complex would be attractive to juniors who are often put off by the rather formal clubs around the world. It would also be a training ground for young professionals because it remains true that the quality of the professional staff very often determines the success of the club. Finally, it would make a wonderful venue for major events and for international festivals along the lines of the Boomerang Cup, which has made such an impact in Melbourne.

INDEX

175